# VANCOUVER ISLAND TRIPS

## FOR KAYAKERS

Novices, 16 trips

Intermediates, 22 trips

Advanced, 22 trips

Experts, 22 trips

*The word "kayak" as used in this book includes all whitewater closed-boats: kayaks (K-1s) and decked canoes (C-1s and C-2s).*

## FOR CANOEISTS

Novices, 2 trips

Intermediates, 8 trips

Experts, 15 trips

*The words "open-canoe" and "open-Canadian canoe" as used in this book refer to a boat without a deck and which is commonly called a canoe.*

## FOR RAFTERS

Novices, 9 trips

Intermediates, 10 trips

Advanced, 10 trips

*The word "raft" as used in this book refers to an inflatable open-boat that has a great deal of flotation.*

Betty Pratt-Johnson

# WHITEWATER TRIPS

## for Kayakers, Canoeists and Rafters on Vancouver Island

The First in a Series of Five Guidebooks
Covering 157 Whitewater Trips in
British Columbia and Washington

**Gordon Soules Book Publishers Ltd., Vancouver/London**
**Pacific Search Press, Seattle**

Canadian Cataloguing in Publication Data

Pratt-Johnson, Betty.
    Whitewater Trips for Kayakers, Canoeists
    and Rafters on Vancouver Island

Includes index.
Bibliography: p.
ISBN 0-919574-67-X (Soules)
ISBN 0-914718-90-8 (Pacific Search)

1. White-water canoeing — British Columbia — Vancouver Island — Guide-books. 2. Canoes and canoeing — British Columbia — Vancouver Island — Guide-books. 3. Rafting (Sports) — British Columbia — Vancouver Island — Guide-books. 4. Rivers — British Columbia — Vancouver Island — Recreational use — Guide-books. 5. Vancouver Island (B.C.) — Description and travel — Guide-books.
I. Title. GV776.15B7P72 1983      917.11'34      C83-091396-3

Library of Congress Catalog Card Number: 83-26190

Published in Canada, Great Britain, and the United States:
**Gordon Soules Book Publishers Ltd.**      **Pacific Search Press**
Canadian Address:                                          222 Dexter Avenue North
C302-355 Burrard Street                                 Seattle, Washington 98109
Vancouver, B.C.                                               U.S.A.
Canada V6C 2G6

British Address:
42/45 New Broad Street
London EC2 M1QY
England

Cover design by Chris Bergthorson
Typeset in Canada by Domino-Link Graphic Communications Ltd.
Printed and bound in Canada by Hignell Printing Limited

## Photographic and Topographic Map Credits

Photographs in this book were taken by the author except those credited below:

Front cover by Bruce Holland; Burnt Bridge Drop on Koksilah River with late November riverflow of 19 m³/s (670 cfs). Brian Henry is in the orange kayak, and Joe McGeragle in the blue one, both of Victoria

Page 28 (bottom photo), Rob Lesser by Dane Wray

Pages 35, 36, and 51, John Pratt-Johnson

Pages 57 (top photo) and 58, Diana Slater

Pages 73 and 113, Government of British Columbia Air Photos

Page 97, Rob Lesser

Back cover, Peter Vassilopoulos

    The map on page 71 has been reproduced, with permission of Energy, Mines and Resources Canada, from the National Topographic System map sheet 92L/8 © 1976 Her Majesty the Queen in Right of Canada.

*Dedicated to . . .*
*the very special people*
*who fished me from many rivers,*
*then paddled with me again*

# ACKNOWLEDGMENTS

Many people have helped me in creating this five-book series, of which the Vancouver Island edition is the first one. I am grateful to each person who had a part in it, and for each pleasure shared.

My biggest thanks go to my husband John for his loyal support of all my kayaking tours, and for his incredible patience during the subsequent period of research and writing. Another very big thank-you goes to publisher Gordon Soules for supplying stimulating criticism, enthusiasm, and good humor throughout the past five years; for always encouraging me to create the best possible product, and for assembling a team of experts to achieve it.

Book production has been a rich experience for me, and the people who worked with me on it are as much a part of my memories accompanying this series of books as are the rivers and surf sites themselves. Special thanks to graphics designer Kerry Jackson for taking time to work with me in developing the design for the access maps, and for her impeccable execution of the maps; and to Donna Longpre, who calmly guided me through the often-exasperating experience of putting my drafts onto computer floppy disks from which typesetting was done automatically.

Thanks to Brian Creer for guiding me on my first river run and for his friendly yelling of directions; to Peter Marshall for his laid-back pool instruction; to Geoff Evans for *showing* our class, as well as *telling* us, that we should climb from our boats to scout, and for introducing us to ocean surfing; to Ben Lemke for not only laughing and fishing me from many rivers when I started paddling, but also for teaching me how to calculate gradients, how to obtain riverflow information, and — most important of all — for helping me to formulate my river philosophy, which is that boating is for sheer fun.

Thanks also to Bev Ramey and Mike Kelly for encouraging me during our many hours practicing the Eskimo roll; to Colin Coe for being a very special paddling buddy since we met at our first pool session; to Mike Bohn for being a good kayaking companion since we met at our first Vancouver Kayak Club outing; to Steve Schleicher for always being ready to paddle during winter as well as summer; and to Willy Paffenholz, who led me down many rivers when I was a novice kayaker and later presented me with the first paddle that he had made as a very tangible acknowledgment of my "graduation". He gave it to me at the take-out after we had kayaked the Thompson River to Lytton. When using that treasured paddle, I still feel the glow from the Thompson — just as the glow from my first Capilano River run returns when talking with Walter Buchmuller, because Walter recalls the aura surrounding me when he met our group coming off the river that day.

I am indebted to Klaus Streckmann for teaching me about river exploration; and to Canadian-kayak-team coach Edna Hobbs, who has always been ready to listen, to respond, and to encourage me, as has Bill Ramey, safety chairman of the Whitewater Canoeing Association of British Columbia. Bill read the entire manuscript several times during its many stages of revision, and I am extremely grateful to him for the energy he gave in helping me to develop a book that not only provides a useful series of technical facts and figures, but also conveys the "go for it" aspect of whitewater boating.

Jack Wainwright, chairman of Canoe Sport British Columbia and an avid open-canoeist, also read the complete manuscript and helped me to round out the information relating to open-canoeists, as did Iain Fisher, past chairman of the Whitewater Canoeing Association of British Columbia and a whitewater kayaking and open-canoeing instructor. Peter Turje provided important information and technical references about rafts and rafting.

The following boaters in Washington State also supplied valuable input: Jim Greenleaf, who is very active in local boating circles and paddles open canoes and kayaks; Kathy Greenleaf, an open-boater and C-1 paddler; watersports equipment dealers Lee and Judy Moyer; boatbuilder Dan Ruuska; and kayaker, rafter, and friend-to-all-paddlers-from-all-places Royce Ward.

Warm thanks to Oliver Nagy of the Water Survey of Canada for providing an invaluable fund of information about riverflow and the measurement of it, and to Orest Chorney of the same office for additional help. I obtained snowpack data from Hal Coulson and Dave Thompson of the provincial Ministry of Environment, as well as information regarding ocean currents from Mike Woodward of the Canadian Hydrographic Service.

I greatly appreciate the moral support and practical guidance given by Bev Ramey, Peter Turje, Gordon Elliott, Jan Bain, and Steve Schleicher when I started to work on the access maps, as well as much information for these maps from Hisao Matsuo and Lidia Rossi of the provincial Ministry of Forests, and assistance from Maureen Wilson, head of the Map Division of The University of British Columbia.

Larry Monterey of the provincial Ministry of Lands, Parks and Housing generously supplied camera-ready international symbols of kayakers, canoeists, and rafters for the locator maps;

Gordie Harris at MAPS-B.C. acquainted me with the vast array of topographic maps and air photos available to the public; the staff of the Language and Literature Division at Vancouver Public Library responded to my many questions; Ed Granirer helped me to decide how to round out the figures to best express both metric and imperial measures; and Greg Fee checked my calculations on gradients.

Vancouver Island people were extremely hospitable and helpful — and a source of much fun. Special thanks to Brian Fuhr for doing more than any other individual to "turn me on" to island rivers and surf, and to sources of information; for paddling that we shared; and for his careful checking of facts in my manuscript. Thanks also to Heidi Krogstad and Kerry Noble, the first islanders I met on an island river who encouraged me to return and paddle with them.

I am grateful to Dane Wray for much excellent paddling, for his endless readiness to "talk paddling" and for his many quotable remarks. And I thank the following islanders for enjoyable days on the rivers and surf: George Allen, Graeme Ashby, Jamie Boulding, Trent Bollinger, David Gerry, Penny Hasell, Barry Hubberstey, David Iannone, Jill Sampson, Jim Tivey, and Owen Williams.

Thanks also to the following islanders for their hospitality: Francie Allen, Myrna and Jim Boulding, Elie Bowles, Mabel Fleetwood, Cathy Hall, Babbie McSporran, and Kathleen Yates; and to other islanders for advice and information: Rick Axford, Joy and Bill Chalmers, Simon Charlie, John Chittick, Don Cohen, Ed Donald, Joe Duckworth, Jack Fleetwood, John Foster, Tony Gallagher, Larry Hall, Howie Hambleton, Margi and Bob Hay, Brian Henry, Jean Hubbard, Alta Johnstone, Don Lewis, John McCracken, Bill Munn, Barbara Stannard, Geoff Warden, and Jeremy Webb.

The happiest boating tour I have experienced up to now was during ten sunny days in May exploring northern Vancouver Island with my husband John, Ben Lemke, and Klaus Streckmann. Adding to the fun during the first three days of that trip were Jan Bain, Colin Coe, Bev and Bill Ramey, and Steve Schleicher. Two years earlier I had enjoyed being part of a class of beginner kayakers taught by Brian Creer, Mark Creer, and Annie Boulding at Strathcona Park Lodge. Carole Chatt, Dick Coxford, Danusia Kanachowski, Linda Keetley, Patti Lefkos, George Prevost, Brent Reid, Jim Rutter and I referred to ourselves as the "white-knuckle crowd".

Other kayakers with whom I have enjoyed island paddling are Linda Anderson, Tim Biggs, Barb and Geoff Evans, Simon Evans, Jenny and Iain Fisher, Mike Fowler, Chuck McWethy, Jim Mancell, Joe Matuska, Grant Mowatt, Greg Mowatt, Brian Pratt-Johnson, Dick Schut, Mike Scott, Jim Stohlquist, and Chan Zwanzig. Thanks for camping in winter rain, for sharing sunny days, and for bowls of hot chili after paddling.

To all of you — thanks for happy times.

# CONTENTS

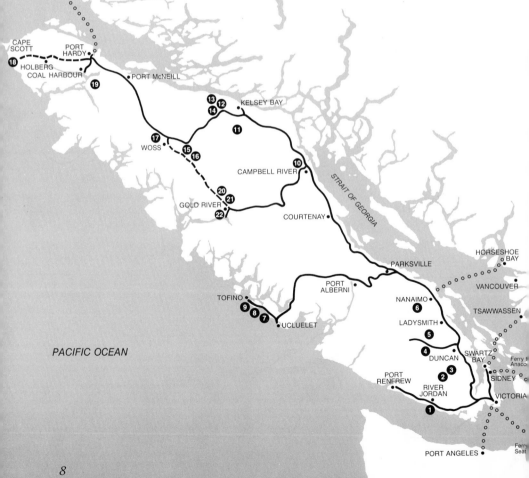

# VANCOUVER ISLAND TRIPS FOR KAYAKERS, CANOEISTS AND RAFTERS

## FOR KAYAKERS

### Novice kayakers, without a guide
❶ River Jordan, Ocean Surf; page 30
❷ Koksilah River, To Burnt Bridge; page 34
❼ Wickaninnish Beach, Ocean Surf; page 54
❽ Long Beach, Ocean Surf; page 56
❾ Cox Bay, Ocean Surf; page 60
❿ Campbell River, Power Plant to Logging Bridge; page 62
⓬ Adam River, To Rooney Lake Junction; page 68
⓱ Nimpkish (Kla-anch) River, Kaipit Creek to Nimpkish Camp; page 84
⓲ San Josef Bay, Ocean Surf; page 88
㉑ Gold River, Middle Section; page 98

### Novice kayakers, with guide
All ten above-named trips and also
❹ Cowichan River, Skutz Falls through Marie Canyon; page 42
❻ Nanaimo River, M&B Bridge to White Rapids Mine; page 50
⓫ White River, Waterfall to First Bridge; page 64
⓰ Nimpkish (Kla-anch) River, Duncan Road Bridge to Woss; page 82
⓳ Marble River, Lake Outlet Falls to Coal Harbour; page 92
㉒ Gold River, The Lower Canyon; page 102

### Intermediate kayakers, without a guide
All sixteen above-named trips and also
❺ Chemainus River, To Copper Canyon; page 46
⓮ Eve River, Montague Creek to Lower Bridge; page 74

### Intermediate kayakers, with guide
All eighteen above-named trips and also
❸ Koksilah River, The Canyon; page 38
⓭ Adam River, The Canyon; page 70
⓯ Davie-Nimpkish Rivers, Island Highway to Woss; page 78
⓴ Gold River, The Upper Canyon; page 96

### Advanced kayakers, without a guide
All twenty-two above-named trips

### Advanced kayakers, with guide
All twenty-two above-named trips

### Expert kayakers
All twenty-two above-named trips

# FOR CANOEISTS

### Novice open-canoeists, without a guide
No trips for this group of paddlers described in this book

### Novice open-canoeists, with guide
**10** Campbell River, Power Plant to Logging Bridge; page 62
**17** Nimpkish (Kla-anch) River, Kaipit Creek to Nimpkish Camp; page 84

### Intermediate open-canoeists, without a guide
The two above-named trips and also
**2** Koksilah River, To Burnt Bridge; page 34
**4** Cowichan River, Skutz Falls through Marie Canyon; page 42
**12** Adam River, To Rooney Lake Junction; page 68
**16** Nimpkish (Kla-anch) River, Duncan Road Bridge to Woss; page 82
**21** Gold River, Middle Section; page 98

### Intermediate open-canoeists, with guide
All seven above-named trips and also
**6** Nanaimo River, M&B Bridge to White Rapids Mine; page 50

### Expert open-canoeists
All eight above-named trips and also
**1** River Jordan, Ocean Surf; page 30
**7** Wickaninnish Beach, Ocean Surf; page 54
**8** Long Beach, Ocean Surf; page 56
**9** Cox Bay, Ocean Surf; page 60
**11** White River, Waterfall to First Bridge; page 64
**18** San Josef Bay, Ocean Surf; page 88
**22** Gold River, The Lower Canyon; page 102


# FOR RAFTERS

### Novice rafters, without a guide
**2** Koksilah River, To Burnt Bridge (paddle rafters only); page 34
**4** Cowichan River, Skutz Falls through Marie Canyon; page 42
**10** Campbell River, Power Plant to Logging Bridge; page 62
**12** Adam River, To Rooney Lake Junction (paddle rafters only); page 68
**16** Nimpkish (Kla-anch) River, Duncan Road Bridge to Woss; page 82
**17** Nimpkish (Kla-anch) River, Kaipit Creek to Nimpkish Camp; page 84
**21** Gold River, Middle Section; page 98
**22** Gold River, The Lower Canyon; page 102

### Novice rafters, with guide
All eight above-named trips and also
**11** White River, Waterfall to First Bridge; page 64

### Intermediate rafters, without a guide
All nine above-named trips and also
**6** Nanaimo River, M&B Bridge to White Rapids Mine; page 50

### Intermediate rafters, with guide
All ten above-named trips

### Advanced rafters
All ten above-named trips

*Wrecked Bridge Drop on Davie River*

# COME RUN A RIVER

Running a new river is the greatest thrill to me; however, in a sense every run is new since rivers change. That is the most impressive fact I learned during five unforgettable years of kayaking and gathering information for this five-book whitewater series. Another amazing discovery was that each river has its own character — like a fingerprint. Some I love more than others, but I have enjoyed something about every river I have described.

Because whitewater routes are in constant flux, I do not believe that rapid-by-rapid description is the best way to go. Instead I emphasize the nature of each river to help you select a run suitable to your liking, your skills, and your mood of the day. I direct you to put-in and take-out points; and alert you to the kinds of changes to expect. You then must find your own way down the rivers. It would be misleading — even dangerous — to give particulars about a river as if it were a static thing, because drops can alter drastically from day to day: a tree falls and blocks the stream; floods cut a new path through the woods; boulders are loosened by freezing and thawing, roll into a narrow chute, changing it from Class 4 to 6.

Radical transformations can occur throughout the year, and almost certainly during spring runoff. Thus copious black-and-white detail about rivers engenders a false sense of security, especially so in the minds of beginners who have not yet had a full season to observe that all rivers are alive, that waterways are constantly developing, growing, receding, changing. The safest way to paddle is to assume that the only constant is change.

This guidebook, like others in my where-to-go regional series, is for all paddlers — from novice to expert. Boaters must possess at least basic kayaking, canoeing, or rafting skills and must use discretion when progressing to more difficult runs. Whitewater day-trips at various paddling levels are described, and each guidebook contains information about Class 1, 2, 3, 4, 5, and 6 water. Because I have paddled all of these rivers and ocean-surfing sites, ratings are reasonably consistent. Once you have tried a couple of rivers you will know what to expect.

The guidebooks evolved as my skills increased, and as I kayaked around British Columbia and Washington. Each stretch of water has been chosen because in one way or another it "feels" like a "kayaker's river". When a run is also suitable for canoeists or rafters it is rated for each of these groups of river users too. The ratings were determined after careful consideration. I have assessed the respective capabilities of each craft for the listed rivers based on my many hours in a whitewater kayak, my limited experience in canoes and rafts, and my extensive consultation with canoeists and rafters. In the section on "How to Use This Guidebook" I have briefly defined the skill levels of kayakers, canoeists, and rafters as referred to here.

In the section on "Water to Expect" I have listed the factors that affect the degree of difficulty, particularly within the regions of this series, and have included information on how to interpret the hydrographs. In the main body of the book, I have summed up the rivers: this has been done after my many hours poring over maps, riverflow records, and aerial photographs, and after having paddled all sites described in this series, and more.

Because exploring rivers is my obsession and passion, I can understand how you might be tempted to go beyond the described trips. However, be aware that if exploration is not done carefully it can be dangerous. In addition, be aware that even though I know that, in some instances, an unrunnable section is upstream or downstream from the described runs, I have not written about it here. To do so would imply that all other sections — where warnings have not been given — are safe, and that could be untrue. A limit to the territory covered had to be set, so I restricted myself to writing about the river sections between the listed put-ins and take-outs. Therefore, if you go beyond any of the river runs as described in this series of guidebooks treat it as original exploration.

Every location was reached in an ordinary van or car: a four-wheel-drive vehicle is not required. Access directions are first given to the take-out, then to the put-in, since paddlers usually use two cars and set up shuttle in that order. When shuttling with a motorcycle or bicycle, I find it more comfortable to do the driving before I am wet. For this reason I go to the put-in first and leave our boats there; next I go to the take-out and leave the van, then ride my bike back to the put-in. If you have a shuttle driver, simply go straight to the put-in.

Since both metric and imperial measurements are in use, I include both terminologies in these guidebooks. Access directions, distances of river runs, and shuttle distances are exact. However to make river widths and gradients, heights of waves and waterfalls, and riverflow figures easy to grasp, I have rounded them wherever possible. When this has been done, the imperial measurements are approximate and the metric measurements are precise.

To my knowledge, all terrain crossed in gaining access to rivers and surf sites is public property or else the circumstances under which it is possible to cross the private property are noted. When gaining access beside a bridge, be aware that the usual minimum right-of-way is the old engineers' measure, one chain. This is approximately 20 meters (66 feet). When following the access directions in this series of guidebooks, if you come across any new signs advising that property is private or stating that no trespassing is allowed, please respect them and advise me of them.

The season affects rivers to a greater extent than does any other factor. However, there is always available paddling in one area or another of British Columbia and Washington. This five-book series begins with descriptions covering Vancouver Island where paddling is especially good in winter and where you can paddle year-round. Then the books in the series move through the seasons, build as the rivers themselves build, because of their rain-fed, snow-runoff, and glacial-melt sources. In early spring, go to the greater Vancouver, Whistler, Fraser Valley, Okanagan, and Thompson River regions; in summer, to the West and East Kootenays; then in autumn to the Cariboo, Chilcotin, and along the Yellowhead Route. Enjoy another full-circle year of paddling throughout the State of Washington.

Although I have kayaked every site described in the series, it was not possible to experience each one in every season; thus I have enriched my firsthand knowledge with input from local paddlers in each area. As a result, these guidebooks are a composite of knowledge. And they are much more than directories of where to put in and take out; they provide what kayakers, canoeists, and rafters need to know in order to decide where to paddle, when.

Quantity of snowpack, warm rain in spring, and summer sunshine on glaciers are all important considerations. The above details represent some of the most essential information in each book, but there is still a great deal more: Play spots? Waterfalls and weirs to watch for? Campsites? Wild berries? Fossils, jade, gold? Practical facts and clues to fun are sprinkled throughout the descriptions; yet much has been left for you to discover.

And much much more than rivers and surf are in this five-book series. Kayaking has led me to many remote places that were new to me and made me aware of wildlife I had never noticed: tiger lilies, lupines and roses; a black bear swimming across a stream; bright spring-green circles of algae swirling lazily on the surface of a hot spring — all of which I have seen either from the river or after paddling.

And beyond the guidebooks? The whitewater experience is more than rivers; more than mountains and scenery and wildlife. When you get out and paddle, you too will find that one of the most priceless and unexpected bonuses that come with rivers is the people you meet on them. Paddlers are as varied, strange, and beautiful as the rivers they run. And you meet "head on": sharing the excitement and demands of whitewater boating helps to cut across the usual reserves; then helps you to mingle; creates special bonds. The urgency of it brings you fully alive so that both you and others soon get to know whoever you really are: funny, sad, whatever. Boating both peels off false layers and fills your life — with adventure, challenges, wilderness, friends. But perhaps the greatest miracle of all about paddling is that no path is left on rivers; and if we are careful while alongside them, no record of our presence will change the scene for generations to come.

Whitewater boating is a wonderful recreation: on every trip I see "one more" tributary that I want to explore. And when studying topographic maps at home, I see "one more" river with an inviting gradient. The problem is not in finding places to paddle in this incredibly water-rich part of the world; for me, the problem is knowing when to stop. There seems no limit to the potential for discovery, and the more we spread onto new rivers, the more uncluttered and free the old standbys will be — even as the fraternity of boaters inevitably increases.

Exciting water is everywhere to be found. Come now with me to these rivers and surf sites, then push off on your own. And each time you do — whether using this guidebook, whether exploring or repeating a favorite river with friends — paddle every one as if it were a new river. It is.

# HOW TO USE THIS GUIDEBOOK

## LOCATOR MAPS

The location of each site being described is pinpointed by the white number within the black circle on the locator map. To help you reach each site, see Whitewater Information Source 1 (page 106) listing tourist information of interest to boaters: road maps, ferries, campgrounds and accommodations, and facilities. The other important information on the locator map is the symbol or symbols indicating who the site is suitable for: kayakers, open-canoeists, rafters.

This symbol indicates that the trip is for kayakers:

This symbol indicates that the trip is for open-canoeists:

This symbol indicates that the trip is for rafters:

## SKILLS

"Excitement enhances, but fear kills it," one kayaker says of whitewater boating. In other words, it is a matter of matching your skills with the demands.

The first point in my description of each site is the expertise necessary to enjoy it. Any closed-boater (kayaker or C-1 or C-2 paddler), open-canoeist, or rafter with basic skills should be able to paddle the easiest rivers described in every one of the five guidebooks in this series. Then progress. A balanced selection of easy, medium, and difficult runs is included in each regional book. For brevity, in the thumbnail sketch listing titled "Who" I have used only the three terms: "kayakers", "open-canoeists", and "rafters". The term "kayakers", as used here, includes persons paddling decked canoes as is explained in the following section on "Boats", and in the section titled "Definitions of Boaters' Skill Levels". See the glossary (page 118) for definition of more special terms used in this guidebook.

Every river-run and ocean-surfing-site description incorporates the best of current knowledge for your safety. All information has been checked by one or more experienced kayakers, canoeists, and rafters, as well as by myself. But this book is not meant to teach you how to paddle: proper training is required before using it. See Whitewater Information Source 2 (page 108) for listings of clubs and courses where you can learn to paddle and where you can meet people to do it with. See Whitewater Information Source 3 (page 110) for listings of books, magazines, and pamphlets containing "how-to" information on techniques, tactics, and equipment.

I cannot stress too strongly that the listed trips are meant only for boaters who can "read" water and who have learned the whitewater skills specific to their particular craft. Warning: rafts are very "forgiving". Therefore, rafters are tempted to progress to more and more difficult water before mastering rowing, recovery and rescue, and especially tactical skills. Furthermore, rafting is so deceptively comfortable: you start out warm. You may go onto the river unprepared for a long swim — without an adequate life jacket for buoyancy in big water, or without a wet suit for buoyancy and warmth.

Should you succumb to the siren song of whitewater rafting without the essential preparation, when your first emergency arises you could already be in extremely heavy water and in a perilous situation such as broaching and wrapping around a rock. Or you could flip, find yourself swimming, with gear scattered, and no companions nearby to pick you up. You could find yourself in trouble with no routines for what to do next and becoming hypothermic if not wearing a wet suit.

These scenarios are less likely to happen to someone learning to kayak because a beginner can tip accidentally in a swimming pool prior to even reaching the river: closed-boaters are wet from the start. Probably someone learning to paddle an open-canoe also would not get too far before becoming acutely aware that precautions must be taken and skills must be acquired; I have come across many smashed canoes wrapped around rocks and caught beneath logjams on easy streams. But rafts are potentially dangerous because of the false sense of security often gained from them — rafting looks so easy.

If you are going to kayak, canoe, or raft, find some way to learn the necessary skills, obtain equipment, and find people to paddle with through a club or course. Then go practice on easy water, and advance in stages. Gradually bite off one bigger bit of water; keep extending yourself. Increase your skills until you and your boat become part of the river. Skill cannot be measured by the number of years you have been paddling. It can only be measured by the variety of whitewater situations you have encountered and learned to cope with *in your craft*. Just because you kayak does not mean you can canoe. Because you can canoe, it does not mean that you can raft. And vice versa. Some whitewater skills cross over. That is, if you "read" water for one type of boating, it helps. But then you must master strokes, emergency recovery and rescue routines, and river-running strategies. Each type of boat has its own disciplines: learn them.

# BOATS

All sites are rated for suitability considering the limitations of each craft: closed-boat, open-canoe, raft.

**1. Closed-boats, including whitewater kayaks (K-1s) and decked canoes (C-1s and C-2s),** can be used on all sites described in the guidebook series: they are highly maneuverable; require very little water to float; are narrow enough to slip between an opening 80 centimeters (31 inches) wide; and are covered with a spray deck so they can go through turbulent water.

**2. Open-canoes** are more difficult to maneuver than closed-boats, especially when paddled by two persons, because there is no central pivot-point; usually they require more water to float, and since normally they are not covered, they can run waves only up to 1 meter (3 feet) high. Open-canoes can handle heavier water when paddled solo by highly skilled individuals.

**3. Rowing rafts and paddle rafts** to be used on whitewater rivers Class 4 and over must be of professional type: I have in mind a 4- to 5-meter (13- to 16-foot) boat with 43-centimeter (17-inch) tube diameter or more and equipped with a rowing frame. It is assumed that rivers to be rowed will have passages at least 3 meters (10 feet) wide, and it must be possible to make a short, uncomplicated, direct shot through them with oars shipped. If a complicated maneuver is required, the passage must be at least 6 meters (20 feet) wide. Paddle rafts are more suitable than rowing rafts on some of the rivers described — particularly the shallow, rocky streams. However, some paddle rafters are skilled on big water and may therefore choose to use paddles instead of oars on all occasions. The choice between paddles and oars depends a great deal on what you are used to. Beware of less sturdy "rubber duckies", inflatable tenders with built-in rubber oarlocks, and various other inflatables not designed for whitewater rivers. Class 3+, 4, and 5 water is runnable only in tough rowing rafts or in tough paddle rafts equipped with high-quality oars or paddles of adequate length and blade size.

The other limitations I have carefully considered are maneuverability, weight, and bulk. Therefore, rivers known to contain many sweepers, logjams, and other debris are considered unsuitable for rafting, as are runs with difficult portages. Flash rivers rated here for rafts can be too rocky to run at low levels, but are fun for rafting when the water's up. Use riverflow profiles, guidelines and on-the-spot judgment to determine when to go.

# TOPOGRAPHIC MAPS, TIDE TABLES, AIR PHOTOS

The topographic map or maps covering the area of each river run are listed in the site descriptions to encourage you to use them: much can be learned by studying maps. However, paddlers must also be aware that many details are not included on topographic maps — sometimes vital information like the 60-meter (200-foot) waterfall on the Adam River (see page 71 of the Vancouver Island book). Never believe that a map is the final total picture of what you will find on a river. Keep your senses alive while you are paddling — and believe *them*.

Topographic maps, or "topos", with contour lines show land elevations and are most commonly used to predict where the greatest descent will probably occur. But more than that can be seen on them. Difficulty, for example, is determined by a combination of vertical drop, the river narrowing and bending, volume of water, obstacles in the riverbed, and steepness of banks. You can read a lot of this on "topo" maps. You can learn a great deal about surrounding terrain and about the character of a river.

With maps, big is not always better. Both large-scale and small-scale "topos" can be very useful. First, study a small-scale map to orient yourself; one of either the 1:500,000 or the 1:1,000,000 series will give you an overview of an enormous chunk of country. You can see entire watersheds. Then, for detail, look at the largest-scale map you can find; see canyons, braided sections, chutes, marshes, and head walls.

In describing each river run, I have noted the names and numbers of the largest-scale topographic map, or maps, covering the site. From those numbers you can also easily find the smaller-scale maps for the same location.

For ocean-surfing sites, instead of topographic maps I have noted the relevant tide tables.

Aerial photographs are available for most of the areas described in this five-book series. Air photos are useful for locating waterfalls, for looking into canyons, and for studying rapids before running them. When viewing two adjacent photos through stereoscopic glasses, you get a "3-D" effect and feel as if you are right on the river. A wealth of photos is on file — so many it would be impossible to list all of them that relate to the rivers in these guidebooks. For this reason, research is required to determine which ones to use. See Whitewater Information Source 4 (page 112) to learn how to obtain air photos and topographic maps. "Topos" and air photos are both excellent ways to view rivers in advance. Use them.

# DEFINITIONS OF BOATERS' SKILL LEVELS

## KAYAKERS (CLOSED-BOATERS)

**Novice**: Can handle Class 2 water.

**Intermediate**: Can maneuver under full control in Class 3 water; upon tipping, usually tries to Eskimo roll and is often successful; can guide novice closed-boaters in Class 2.

**Advanced**: Can maneuver under control in Class 4 water; upon tipping, Eskimo rolls successfully almost every time; and can guide intermediate closed-boaters in Class 3.

**Expert**: Can maneuver with finesse and paddle under full control in Class 4 water; upon tipping, Eskimo rolls successfully almost every time. Can handle Class 5 water; and can lead advanced closed-boaters in Class 4.

## OPEN-CANOEISTS

**Novice**: Has successfully paddled calm lakes, but is inexperienced on moving water.

**Intermediate**: Experienced on Class 1 moving water and can handle Class 2.

**Expert**: Can maneuver under control in Class 3 water; and can sometimes successfully run Class 4.

## RAFTERS

**Novice**: Can handle Class 2 water.

**Intermediate**: Can maneuver under full control in Class 3.

**Advanced**: Can maneuver under control in Class 4 water; and can possibly handle Class 5.

# WATER TO EXPECT

As paddlers become more proficient they tend to rate water lower, which is natural, because the water no longer presents the same challenge to them. Sometimes it is also macho — paddlers do not want to admit that a stretch was difficult so the class drops. "When you start making decisions for other people you start rating a river realistically" says a kayak instructor. She's right. I have found that the only time I face up to what the classification of a river really is, is when I ask others to join me. My sense of river rating becomes particularly acute if I am leading. Therefore, when summing up water in these guidebooks I have kept in mind flesh-and-blood friends who possess different levels of skill: I want them to enjoy the river. Can they paddle what's there? Will it push them enough? Will it provide the fun and excitement they want?

Whitewater rivers and ocean-surfing sites are rated according to the International Scale of River Difficulty from Class 1 through Class 6. An idea of the proportion of easy and demanding water you can expect is given. Mandatory portages are noted, and optional portages are mentioned when particular drops are more difficult than the rest of the run.

Also I indicate whether the river consists of steady flow, continuous rapids, or drops and pools, "technical" water or "big" water. If technical, you have to maneuver around rocks or boulders: it is small, tight, and busy. If big, you have to react to surging water — but classification of rivers is not that simple. Volume, gradient, and width of watercourse occur in infinite combinations to create rapids and drops of varying difficulties; details about these points, and other factors that affect the degree of difficulty, are on hydrographs and in the "Guidelines" section. Precise riverflow, or my estimate of it, and the time of year when I paddled the site are in the "Season" section. This information gives an idea of the circumstances my impressions are based on. River ratings are summed up in the "Water to expect" section of each site description.

**Volume**: As volume increases, the potential power of a river increases; but large volume alone does not create difficulty. Rivers come alive when the flow is complicated by variations in gradient and width. In these guidebooks, volume of riverflow is shown on graphs; more about this in the subsequent section entitled "The Hydrograph: A Riverflow Profile".

**Gradient**: As steepness of terrain increases, speed of riverflow does too, all other things being equal (but they never are!), so the degree of difficulty also increases. Gradient, or drop, is expressed in the following way: When a river loses 10 meters (30 feet) of height over a distance of 1 kilometer (0.6 mile), the average gradient is listed as 10 meters/kilometer (55 feet/mile). Remember that gradient figures are only averages; the total vertical descent may be evenly spread out or it may come all in one drop. Remember, too, that incline is only one of several factors that interact to increase the demands of the river.

**Width**: When a river narrows, intensity of flow increases. Constricting canyon walls and the presence of obstacles — rocks, boulders, bridge piers — both decrease channel size. When a river narrows or bends, and if other factors remain the same, difficulty increases. Details of width and gradient are given in the site-description "Guidelines".

---

**PROBABLE DIFFICULTY RATING
AT VARIOUS GRADIENTS ON SMALL-VOLUME RIVERS**

| Water Difficulty | Gradient Up To |
|---|---|
| Easy | 5 meters/kilometer  (25 feet/mile) |
| Moderately Difficult | 10 meters/kilometer  (55 feet/mile) |
| Difficult | 15 meters/kilometer  (80 feet/mile) |
| Very Difficult | 20 meters/kilometer (105 feet/mile)<br>    and greater |

*Note: This does not apply to sections of rivers with extreme constriction nor does it apply to very-large-volume rivers.*

---

**Other factors that increase difficulty**: If the river is remote from any road, if it is an extremely long and tiring paddle, if there is a big chance of sweepers and logs in the river, or if there are special hazards to look out for — such as fishermen's nets suspended over the river — these possible conditions also are mentioned.

Regional conditions you should be aware of are cold water, glacial water, and logs. Most rivers in the area are cold year-round. Come prepared for it, then when you reach a nice warm river in summer, and it's going to be a short run, leave some of your gear in the car. But be ready for cold both in winter and in summer. In addition to being frigid, glacial rivers are also murky, which increases risk because you cannot see what is beneath the surface. And logs can appear on any river.

To counteract cold water and cold weather, the usual year-round garb of the local paddler is a woolen or synthetic pile pullover, a farmer-John or farmer-Jane wet suit, a waterproof paddling jacket, and hard-soled neoprene boots or neoprene socks with high-cut sneakers.

In winter, many paddlers wear nylon pogies or neoprene mitts, neoprene jackets, and wool or neoprene caps under their helmets, as well as carrying thermoses of hot drinks and cigarette lighters or matches to light fires.

Then there are logs — the "X" factor. Logs are not even mentioned in the usual International Scale of River Difficulty definitions, probably because they are less of a problem in other regions of North America and in other parts of the world than they are here. Yet logs are the greatest potential killers on waterways in British Columbia and Washington. Rivers on which they are most likely to be are singled out in the site descriptions, but — and I repeat — be aware that logs can appear on any river and in the ocean surf. When on rivers, carry a throw rope for rescue purposes, and paddle defensively. The best time to hit high water is after the peak of runoff so that no logs are chasing you down the river; do not explore when rivers are muddy, rising fast, and running between the trees. Especially when paddling water new to you, proceed under full control so that you can stop if you see a fallen tree or a logjam; move on only when there is clear passage to two eddies beyond that you are confident you can catch. Know your level of ability. As one kayaker expresses it: "Don't drive beyond your headlights."

Difficulty increases in direct relationship to reaction time required of the boater. Ratings given in the site descriptions are based on the following factors included in the system of classification that is in use throughout the world.

---

## INTERNATIONAL SCALE OF RIVER DIFFICULTY

Class 1: *Very easy*. Moving water with a few riffles and small waves; few or no obstructions.

Class 2: *Easy*. Rapids with waves up to 1 meter (3 feet) high with occasional rocks, boulders, sweepers, or artificial obstructions like bridge piers; clear and wide passages. Some maneuvering required.

Class 3: *Moderately difficult*. Waves either high or irregular, or both; rocks, holes, boulders, logs, or other obstacles with obvious narrow passages. Scouting may be necessary. Considerable maneuvering required.

Class 4: *Difficult*. Powerful irregular waves, boiling eddies, or long rapids. Scouting from shore may be necessary. Skillful precise maneuvering is required within areas containing big hydraulics, or within drops.

Class 5: *Very difficult*. Powerful, unpredictable waves or whirlpools, long violent rapids, or rocks or other obstructions with powerful water on the only line of passage. Scouting from shore is mandatory. Difficult and precise maneuvering required in unpredictable, violent water. In the event of a paddler having to swim, rescue of boater may not be possible; equipment probably will be lost, because conditions make its salvage difficult.

Class 6: *Extraordinarily difficult*. Difficulties of Class 5 are carried to the extreme in Class 6. Because it is very dangerous and because there is such high risk to the boater's life, passage should not be attempted.

---

**Note**: *Extremely cold water in conjunction with any of the above conditions raises the rating by one class. Furthermore, when water is up during runoff it almost always raises the difficulty by at least one class above listed ratings. At high water some rivers become unrunnable.*

The above river-classification system was adapted by the author from the scale of river ratings developed by the American Whitewater Affiliation, and has been officially approved by the Slalom and Wildwater Committee of the International Canoe Federation.

# THE HYDROGRAPH: A RIVERFLOW PROFILE

Riverflow is measured and recorded for many streams. As shown on the tables below, it is expressed in cubic meters per second (m³/s) or cubic feet per second (cfs). When these figures are added up, averaged, and put on a graph, flow patterns become obvious. Seasonal variations and relative volume stand out — both being major factors to consider when planning where to paddle.

I have classified rivers in this series of guidebooks into four categories: small, medium, large, and giant. Apart from the Columbia, Fraser, Thompson, and Skeena, which are so enormous they are in a class alone, all of the rivers fall into the first three categories. Throughout this series the four classifications are identified by different numbers and different sizes of bubbles, as shown on the following graphs:

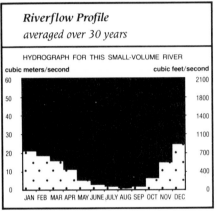

This is a hydrograph for a stream on Vancouver Island that is classified, based on its average monthly flow, as small volume: the Koksilah River.

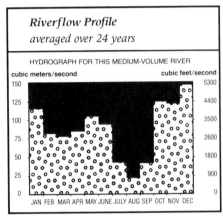

This is a hydrograph for a river on Vancouver Island that is classified, based on its average monthly flow, as medium volume: Gold River.

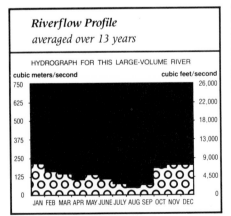

This is a hydrograph for a river on Vancouver Island that is classified, based on its average monthly flow, as large volume: the Nimpkish River.

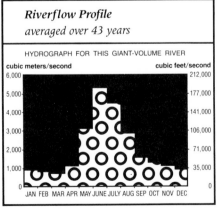

This is a hydrograph for a river that is classified, based on its average monthly flow, as giant volume: the Columbia River (near the Canada-U.S.A. border).

River measurement began in British Columbia in 1911, and in Washington in 1891. Riverflow has been recorded for some rivers ever since that time. For others, data has been collected for a short period; and for still others, there is no information. Individual river records range from part of a year up to 92 years, and there are several water-gauging stations on some rivers.

Whatever information is available from the water-gauging station on a run (or nearest to it upstream or downstream) is included in this guidebook, and the exact time span the discharge is averaged over is noted at the top of each hydrograph. The most accurate assessment of volume is obtained when you know whether a station is within a run, above it, or below it. Therefore water-gauging station locations, both active and inactive, are shown on the access maps; when a measuring location is off of the map, an indication of whether it is upstream or downstream is given, and the distance to it is stated.

Hydrographs depict averages but do not represent any actual year unless one year is the only period of record; rather they give a general indication of what to anticipate. Averages over a longer period probably project more reliably what to expect — but don't count on it. Conditions vary; almost every season is an exception. If there is a big snowpack and spring comes slowly, runoff goes on and on. If hot weather or warm rain hits, rivers rage.

Rivers rise and fall differently every year; however, certain patterns do emerge. It is instantly obvious which are "winter" rivers that are dependent upon rain; which are "spring" runoff rivers; and which are "late summer" glacial-fed waterways rising with hot summer sun. Some rivers are stabilized by large lakes above them that collect precipitation and delay reaction time, thus enabling them to maintain fairly constant flow throughout the year. In most cases it is possible to guess which rivers are moderated by lakes by scanning profiles. If riverflow is controlled by a dam, another flow pattern will result depending on the purpose of regulation: for power source, irrigation, drinking-water supply, industrial use, or to maintain flows for fish in low-water periods. Hydrographs provide much information to paddlers; however it is impossible to distinguish flash rivers from the graphs because high daily peaks simply do not appear in a monthly average.

Flash rivers are up one day, down the next. The only prudent way to plan for them is to watch for rain, then go to the river and take a look. Flash rivers are singled out in the site-description section under "Season". To learn more about daily flows on flash rivers, and other rivers, study government surface-water-data annuals. See Whitewater Information Source 5 (page 115) to learn where to obtain the annuals and where to obtain more detail on riverflow. Also in Whitewater Information Source 5 see the table of maximum recorded discharges at each water-gauging station referred to in the trip descriptions in this guidebook: astonishing figures. Practical too. One professional rafter told me that during peak months he always looks at the maximum recorded flow before going onto a river ". . . because *that's* [the maximum recorded discharge] what *could* happen!". For this reason, and for all short-term planning, it is extremely helpful to have precise up-to-the-minute flow information so you know whether it's worth heading to the river.

Current readings are available for a limited number of streams by telephoning prior to going to the river, as noted in Whitewater Information Source 5. Upon arriving at some rivers, instructions in "Guidelines" direct you so that you can find the staff gauge and check out levels for yourself. At still others, informal measuring devices are useful: an arbitrary scale painted on a weir, water over bridge piers, or water covering old pilings.

All known aids to determine if riverflow is within a favorable range are included in the trip descriptions. And don't forget to use hydrographs too, because they are still the best aid for long-term planning. But if you arrive at the put-in and, in spite of all efforts to predict, you find the water level is not favorable for you or your boat — go home!

# ACCESS MAPS

The access maps in this guidebook, and in others in the series, are primarily intended to show you the way to the river. They are not intended as maps of the river rapids. However, I have noted on them some named drops and canyons. Also campgrounds, facilities, and points of interest. In addition, I have noted obvious "fixed" danger points such as waterfalls, weirs, and dams that are within described runs; but I have made no attempt to map hazards upstream or downstream from described runs.

Pointers to put-ins and take-outs indicate the easiest paths to and from the water, so you will find it useful to note to which part of the riverbank they direct you. Then, when on the water, you must choose your own route and proceed under control throughout every run every time, because at any time you may round a bend and come across a fallen tree or a chute that is blocked with boulders. Rivers change.

## ACCESS MAP LEGEND

| | | | |
|---|---|---|---|
| Paved Highway or Paved Secondary Road | ▬▬▬ | Campground | ▲ |
| Gravel Road | - - - - - | Picnic Site | 🛉 |
| Road Bridge | —)(— | Cafe, Store, Pub, Hotel, Restaurant, Information Center | ◇ |
| Trail | .......... | | |
| Footbridge | —Ⅰ— | Dam | →( |
| Railway Tracks | +—+—+—+ | | |
| | | Weir | ⇒ |
| Power Line | _._._._ | | |
| Ferry Route | o o o o o o o | Waterfall | ⇒[ |

*Ocean surfing at Cox Bay*

*Quiet waters beneath cavern
on Marble River*

*Gold River*

# WHAT'S SPECIAL
# ABOUT VANCOUVER ISLAND?

Canyons, undercut caves and waterfalls are found on many of the narrow rain-fed island rivers and the ocean has broad sandy surfing beaches.

Winter is *the* time to paddle; year-round boating is a reality; late summer is the slimmest time — but if you like ocean surfing that takes care of that. When streams everywhere else are frozen solid, water is dashing down rivers on the island. The landscape is low compared with that of other parts of the province. There are few glaciers to sustain flow in late summer; few lakes to moderate high flows. Rivers rise and fall dramatically. Many are flash streams, responding to rain and early snow-melt. All waterways are small or medium volume, except for the Nimpkish River which, despite its large volume, is relatively easy water to negotiate. When rivers are raging, the heaviest water to be found on the island is in the lower canyon of Gold River. Records for it show an average riverflow for May of 109 $m^3/s$ (3850 cfs); a maximum recorded flow of 1890 $m^3/s$ (66,700 cfs) on November 13, 1975. It can be impressive.

Two peaks occur on Vancouver Island rivers: the biggest is during autumn rains when much debris is picked up and scattered down them; the second during spring runoff. Enthusiastic local paddlers take advantage of both peaks and sponsor whitewater races in spring and fall: a "totally-for-fun" April Fools' Day race on the Nanaimo is soon followed by more serious competition on the Cowichan. The latter event frequently is used for provincial team selection. During October, ocean-surfing championships are held at Long Beach on the West Coast; and the whitewater racing season climaxes in the north central island at races sponsored by Strathcona Park Lodge with a marvelous mix of exciting whitewater paddling, comfort in the sauna, mellow meals — then square-dance the night away.

Scattered across the island is a wonderful array of rivers and surf sites as beautiful as their names. The list of places to paddle is a rich conglomeration of North American Indian and biblical origin: River Jordan village near Victoria is the first site location described in this guidebook; Adam River flows into Eve River in the northern island wilderness; between them, the Koksilah, Chemainus, and Nanaimo Rivers are named after smaller tribes of the Great Cowichan Band. The family tree of the Cowichan, the family tree of man. Vancouver Island — a place of beginnings.

# RIVER JORDAN
## *Ocean Surf*

**Who:** All kayakers on 1-meter (3-foot) high waves; intermediate and advanced kayakers with Eskimo roll on larger ones. Expert open-canoeists on waves up to 1 meter (3 feet) high. No rafters

**Water to expect:** Varies from flat water up to 4-meter (13-foot) high waves; sporadic surf. Gently shelving cobble beach

**Length of run:** Depending on wave height, surf breaks from at least 100 meters (300 feet) offshore to the beach

**Shuttle one way:** None required

**Why go:** Easy-to-reach "clean break", an interesting community, a view; marine mammals and birds.

When the surf's up, this "break" ranks among the top four in North America according to board surfers who migrate to River Jordan in winter. They like it because when the surf is really large there is an excellent rip current to ride out at the river mouth where waves seldom break. Paddle out on this protected channel to "the green" (smooth water beyond the surf break). No walking to reach water's edge. Since this is primarily a winter site, the tide is in when you kayak and there is no beach. Just step from your parking spot over a narrow jumble of silvery logs to the water. Waves roll in to a 300-meter (980-foot) wide strip of waterfront road in town; non-paddlers can sit inside at The Breakers Restaurant and watch you surf.

There was no road to the River Jordan settlement until 1918, but it was a thriving community from 1910 through the 1920s. At its industrial peak, some pioneers came for logging, others for copper mining, many to build a hydroelectric dam. In the 1950s and 1960s, there was a resurgence of copper mining. Today only a few people remain, mostly to work at the dam; the current census has dropped to about 70. However, I suspect that each person living there now is an intriguing individual: residents tell of a postman who refused to deliver a letter because it was addressed to Jordan River (the river) rather than River Jordan (the village).

The scene is magnificent: on a clear day you can see across Juan de Fuca Strait to the snow-capped Olympic Peninsula. Gray whales, sea lions, harbor seals, otters, and bald eagles are seen from the point; we also saw a California quail darting among the cobblestones.

**Tide Tables:** *Canadian Tide & Current Tables, Volume 5, Juan de Fuca and Georgia Straits*; refer to Sooke daily tables.

**Facilities:** The Breakers Restaurant across the road. Jordan River Picnic Park at the point: fresh water to wash your gear; pit toilets and picnic tables. China

**Season:** Fall through spring; from September through June. Best in winter. Occasional and unpredictable. We kayak-surfed it in mid-January with ½-meter (1½-foot) high waves; a week later waves were 3 meters (10 feet) high

*Pogies for warm hands*

Beach Provincial Park often is the site of another good surf break. When the ocean front at River Jordan is flat, check it out. Go west 4.0 kilometers (2.5 miles) to the parking lot for China Beach; then a 15-minute walk down-

*River Jordan*

*Inside The Breakers Restaurant, picnic park across water*

hill beneath tall trees to the sand. Camping, for a fee during peak season, back toward Victoria; from River Jordan go 10.1 kilometers (6.3 miles) to French Beach Provincial Park.

**Guidelines:** Kayak-surfers are usually out in front of The Breakers Restaurant; board-surfers off the point at River Jordan. Beware of logs tossing in the surf, as at all sites in the region. When surfing, it is advisable to have toggles on your kayak in case you swim; they will save your hands from being twisted in the grab loops. And timing? How does one try to predict the surf? Wind, weather, and tide affect it: best on an incoming tide. However, "Wind is everything to it" according to an experienced local kayak-surfer who says tide is the least important consideration here: "Southeast wind kills the waves; west wind is good; or preferably *no* wind. Watch the television weather maps: low pressure in the Gulf of Alaska usually is followed by surf. Once up, it might last several hours. Or several days."

Although rare and unreliable, River Jordan is one of the best surfing sites for those who are lucky or willing to wait for the waves to come up. Throughout winter it averages only two or three good days each week; a superb day each month. It's risky to plan a trip especially for it, but worth the hour's drive to see it, or a call to check on it when you are nearby. For on-the-spot surf information after 10 a.m. telephone "Mac" MacDonald at The Breakers Restaurant: (604)646-2079.

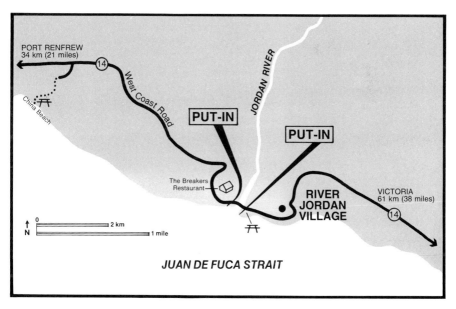

**Access to the put-in:** From Victoria a 1-hour drive: following signs to Sooke, go on Highway 14 (West Coast Road) for 64 kilometers (40 miles) to River Jordan village. Put in either across from The Breakers Restaurant or from the spit off the left riverbank of the Jordan, depending on what the surf is like. The choice will be obvious.

# KOKSILAH RIVER
## *To Burnt Bridge*

**Who:** All kayakers; intermediate and expert open-canoeists; paddle rafters

**Water to expect:** Class 2 with Class 3 chutes (easy to carry around); look at the last two drops to sum up what you want to run. Small volume; steady gradient half the way, then technical

**Length of run:** 6.0 kilometers (3.7 miles); 1½ hours

**Shuttle one way:** 5.1 kilometers (3.2 miles); 10 minutes. Gravel roads

**Season:** Winter and spring runoff; October through April. Responds to

**Why go:** Excellent for Class 2 paddlers who want to try some short Class 3 drops, and for anyone who wants to enjoy a not-too-long scenic paddle through the woods. This shallow river runs through a rock garden; develops into pools; then builds to narrow fun chutes — and you can "take 'em or leave 'em".

Beside the river, an expansive open-parkland feeling beneath huge deciduous trees covered with brilliant spring-green moss. Crooked bare branches hang witch-like over the water. We see some evergreens. Sandy beaches. No houses; only one deserted log cabin. The road is close in case you become cold and want to take out en route, but does not intrude, is not "with you" as you paddle. If you are splashed, it probably will be in the more exciting drops near the end of the run, which helps, because paddling the Koksilah is a "winter thing to do".

**Topographic Map:** 1:50,000 Shawnigan Lake 92B/12.

**Facilities:** Camping is free at undeveloped Koksilah River Provincial Park; room for tents on the bank above the river on the right before you cross Burnt Bridge.

**Guidelines:** Pick a sunny day after heavy rain to paddle the Koksilah. Avoid extremely high water; however, if you make a mistake and the river is too high, you can easily take out at many places along this stretch because the river is close to the road. Gradient on this section averages 9 meters/kilometer (45 feet/mile); width is 10 to 15 meters (30 to 50 feet). Watch for sweepers: we did not see any but they are a potential danger on narrow waterways like this that you paddle shortly after rain.

In the top part, a rock garden. Beyond the power lines, look for Class 3 drops at bedrock ledges: one was 1 meter (3 feet) high and only 2 meters (6 feet) wide. Freezing and thawing may loosen fresh rockfalls which then cascade into the river. Chutes can change. Paddle in control and climb from your boat

rain; a flash river. I paddled it in mid-January with riverflow of 9 m$^3$/s (320 cfs)

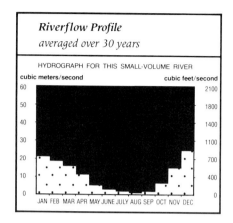

**Riverflow Profile**
*averaged over 30 years*

HYDROGRAPH FOR THIS SMALL-VOLUME RIVER

to scout. You may want to portage some drops, particularly the last one before Burnt Bridge.

Riverflow was 212 m$^3$/s (7500 cfs) on December 14, 1979. This is a flash river — high water could happen to you!

*A chute*

*Warm mitts for winter paddling*

*Boat in bushes, now off to the van*

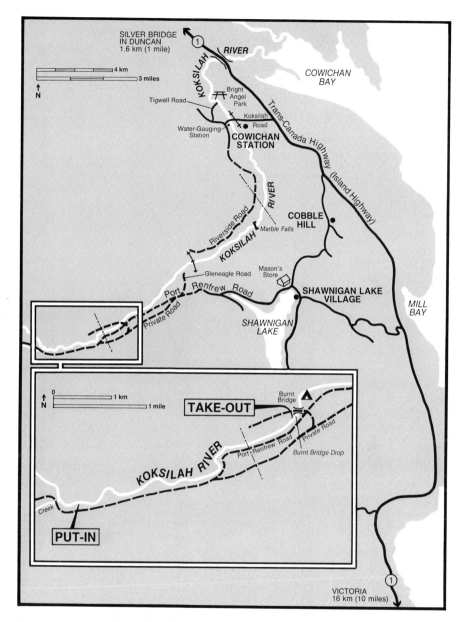

**Access to put-in and take-out:** From Trans-Canada Highway 1 (Island Highway) go via Cobble Hill or Shawnigan Lake village to Port Renfrew Road. Head west on Renfrew Road past Mason's Store with Shawnigan Lake on your left; the road soon becomes gravel. Shortly past Gleneagle Road take the right fork to Burnt Bridge. Across the bridge, there is limited roadside parking near the take-out, which is a scramble through the bushes.

To put in, return across Burnt Bridge and turn right. Head upstream along the south bank of the Koksilah for 5.0 kilometers (3.1 miles). Just before a bridge over a creek, turn right into a large parking area.

# KOKSILAH RIVER
## *The Canyon*

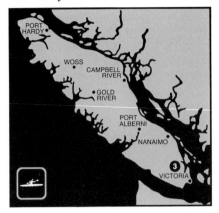

**Who:** Advanced kayakers and guided intermediates; no open-canoeists; no rafters

**Water to expect:** Water to expect: Class 3+ to 4; two Class 4 to 5 drops (difficult to portage) and a mandatory easy portage. Drops and pools through a remote canyon: unpushy at moderate levels (as it was when we paddled it); unrunnable at extremely high levels

**Length of run:** 14.8 kilometers (9.2 miles); 6 hours

**Shuttle one way:** 22.2 kilometers (13.8 miles); 30 minutes. Gravel road

**Why go:** An irresistible combination — at least to me. A spectacular canyon close to the city, yet cut off. And fleeting. Catch it if you can!

**Topographic Map:** 1:50,000 Shawnigan Lake 92B/12.

**Facilities:** Camping is free at undeveloped Koksilah River Provincial Park on the bank above the put-in at Burnt Bridge. Picnicking beneath a magnificent stand of old-growth firs and cedars near the take-out; from Riverside Road continue west 1.1 kilometers (0.7 mile) on Koksilah Road, then turn right into Tigwell Road and follow signs to Bright Angel Provincial Park.

**Guidelines:** The critical variable to anticipate on this one is optimum riverflow: expect it in winter, spring, or fall after torrential downpour for three or four days on an already-watersoaked landscape. Then wait for a couple of days for the water to recede and clear. Flow can become too great, but once at the take-out you can check it. From Cowichan Station Bridge, paddle a short way upstream and look at a staff gauge on your right when facing upstream. For each gauge height there is a corresponding volume of riverflow listed on a rating scale. The reading when we paddled was between 1.1 and 1.2 meters (3.5 and 4.0 feet) indicating flow of 12 m³/s (420 cfs) The river could be run at slightly higher level, but go cautiously. If the gauge had read ½ meter (1½ feet) higher, discharge would have been almost three times as much — a radical change on this small stream. Read the gauge. And believe it! Remember that staff-gauge rating scales for this river, as for others, could change from year to year as the riverbed changes. Before paddling, obtain the current scale from Water Survey of Canada, Suite 502, 1001 West Pender Street, Vancouver, B.C. V6E 2M9, telephone (604)666-3850 after 1 p.m.

The Koksilah run is divided into three parts: warm-up rapids, an intense canyon, and tranquil farmland. When putting in at Burnt Bridge, remember that Class 1 riffles soon develop into Class 3 drops with pools between, then steep narrow chutes. Along the riverbanks, homes are scattered among cedars

for 5.0 kilometers (3.1 miles); the rest is pavement

**Season:** October through April; best chance during spring runoff. A flash stream: responds to rain. If warm rain falls on low, big snowpack, it could be dangerous. However, riverflow can be determined before putting in: see "Guidelines" below. I paddled it in mid-November with riverflow of 12 m³/s (420 cfs)

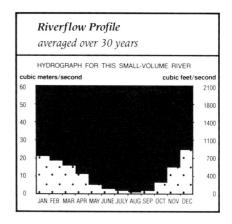

*Riverflow Profile*
*averaged over 30 years*

HYDROGRAPH FOR THIS SMALL-VOLUME RIVER

cubic meters/second — cubic feet/second

JAN FEB MAR APR MAY JUNE JULY AUG SEP OCT NOV DEC

as far as the immense wooden railway trestle, beyond which you reach the point of no return. Paddlers who want out can climb a steep trail beside the trestle on river left; then walk five minutes along the railroad grade to Riverside Road. Past the trestle you are committed to paddle or portage through the narrow steeply walled canyon. Three extreme drops are downstream: two are Class 4+ to 5; the third is Class 5 or 6. To portage the first two you must climb steep, slippery rocks and wooded banks; we scrambled around them on "river right". From the deepest part of the canyon you might see Solo Deo Franciscan Monastery high on a north bank. You are coming out of the canyon when at Marble Falls which is unrunnable because of a fish ladder.

*Above Burnt Bridge*

Recognize the falls when you see a concrete structure midstream. The portage around is short and easy over rocks on the right of the rounded sloping cascade. After that a couple of "lightweight" rapids to run; then drift along on slow water beneath overhanging branches of trees that interlace to form a filagree tunnel — a quiet conclusion among the willows.

River width averages 10 to 15 meters (30 to 50 feet) in the top part. Between trestle and power lines the river narrows to half of that, or less, depending on volume of flow. Past the power lines, the river spreads. Gradient overall averages 7 meters/kilometer (35 feet/mile); in the canyon, 11 meters/kilometer (60 feet/mile). Dangers? Fallen trees blocking narrow chutes are an ever-present possibility on a narrow river like this which is kayaked only infrequently after large rains. Cold weather in winter, a long run, and inaccessibility at the most difficult chutes — with boat-breaking potential — and you have a serious Class 4 run. Take matches, hot drinks, and materials to mend boats.

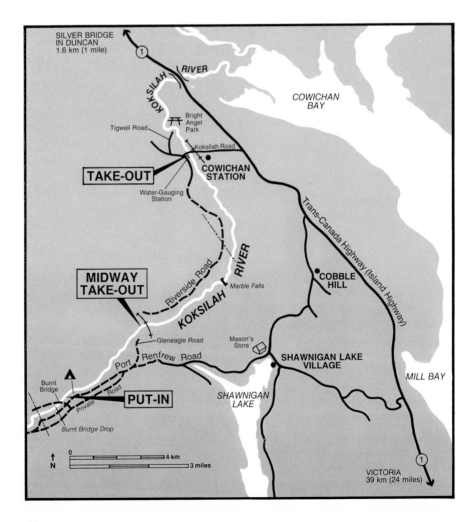

*In the canyon: climbing from boats to portage*

**Access to take-out and put-in:** Turn off Trans-Canada Highway 1 (Island Highway) onto Koksilah Road which is 6.4 kilometers (4.0 miles) south of the Silver Bridge over the Cowichan in Duncan and 3.7 kilometers (2.3 miles) north of Cobble Hill Road. Go west on Koksilah Road. Just past the railway underpass at Cowichan Station you reach the take-out bridge. Across it and just before Riverside Road, there is room for two or three cars to park at the take-out.

For the put-in, return to the highway. Go south and turn right up Cobble Hill Road. At Renfrew Road turn right and head west past Mason's Store with Shawnigan Lake on your left; the road soon becomes gravel. Shortly past Gleneagle Road take the right fork to Burnt Bridge.

---

A midway take-out in case someone wants to climb out at the railway trestle is a 15-minute drive beyond Cowichan Station. Head up Riverside Road which soon becomes gravel logging road. Immediately after passing beneath power lines you reach a crossroad; continue straight and measure the distance carefully. When at 6.6 kilometers (4.1 miles), cross a culvert, bear right, and in 1.3 kilometers (0.8 mile) park at a lay-by on the left beside an overgrown railway grade. Turn left and walk south along the grade for 5 minutes to the trestle over the canyon.

Since the turn of the century, many small copper mines have been worked near the Koksilah. Above this old railway grade, mining is still going on at Queen of Sheba, Bluebell, and King Solomon Mines.

---

When on Riverside Road, watch for logging trucks. Drive with your headlights on.

# COWICHAN RIVER
## *Skutz Falls through Marie Canyon*

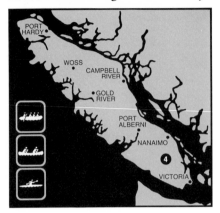

**Who:** Intermediate and advanced kayakers; expert open-canoeists; intermediate and advanced rafters. At low levels, also guided novice kayakers, intermediate open-canoeists, and novice rafters

**Water to expect:** Class 2 and 3; at high water, some Class 4. Medium volume; steady gradient

**Length of run:** 3.9 kilometers (2.4 miles); 3 hours

**Shuttle one way:** 2.7 kilometers (1.7 miles); 5 minutes. Gravel road

**Why go:** An infamous hole at the S-Bend, Double Whammy, and The Last Drop. Beautiful canyon walls curve up around you as you play on the aqua-blue Cowichan: good paddling for a short, short shuttle.

Throughout most of the year there is water in this popular river which is enjoyed by everyone from novices to experts. During runoff it can provide Class 4 challenges. At low levels it is a favorite training river for Victorians. Since 1975, annual whitewater kayak races have been held on it, and it is often designated as provincial-team-selection slalom. The Cowichan is a safe fun place for almost all kayakers at almost all times because it is relatively "clean", or free from sweepers, and there are good surfing waves, holes, and drops.

Other boaters paddle it too: the Cowichan Band has long been active on this river which bears their tribal name. From the turn of the century until the mid-1930s, they honored prominent visitors by taking them in Indian dugouts from Cowichan Lake through Marie Canyon to Duncan. In 1929 they treated Governor General of Canada Lord Willingdon and Lady Willingdon to this spectacular wilderness run.

The canyon remains unspoiled today: no homes are seen from it; instead there is a wonderful selection of wooded campsites alongside.

Non-boaters also enjoy the river. The Indian meaning of Cowichan is "the warm land": in summer the water is warm too, and swimmers are in it. A hiking trail developed by and for anglers is alongside this run. The fish ladder around the falls is an interesting sight, and the river is well known for superb salmon and steelhead trout fishing. When the B.C. Wildlife Federation presented a proposal to the provincial government for a "Wild, Scenic and Recreational River" in 1972, its choice for the category of recreational river was the Cowichan.

**Topographic Map:** 1:50,000 Duncan 92B/13.

**Facilities:** Beautiful free campsites with picnic tables, pit toilets, and fire rings

**Season:** October to June. Best after runoff, usually in April or May, and after rain. Rain-fed and snow-melt; stabilized by the lake above. I paddled it in early October and mid-January with riverflows of 28 m³/s (990 cfs) and 66 m³/s (2330 cfs)

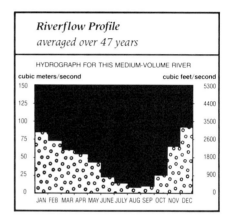

*Riverflow Profile*
*averaged over 47 years*

HYDROGRAPH FOR THIS MEDIUM-VOLUME RIVER

cubic meters/second        cubic feet/second

| | |
|---|---|
| 150 | 5300 |
| 125 | 4400 |
| 100 | 3500 |
| 75 | 2600 |
| 50 | 1800 |
| 25 | 900 |
| 0 | 0 |

JAN FEB MAR APR MAY JUNE JULY AUG SEP OCT NOV DEC

are scattered among the trees along the shuttle route between Skutz Falls and Marie Canyon.

**Guidelines:** There is always action at the S-Bend, but it can be sneaked. The longest and most difficult rapid is beyond the railway trestle: a series of standing waves called Double Whammy. Two parts to it: good intermediate kayakers can surf the first set, then hit the eddy in the middle of it for more fun surfing.

Play spots throughout the run are most numerous when the river is medium level, from 40 to 60 m³/s (1400 to 2100 cfs) At flood, much of the river "washes out" and there are few play waves as well as few eddies — and not many banks to pull out on in the steeply walled canyon. However, at high levels the entire run can be scouted from the water; the Class 3 and 4 "things

*Below Skutz Falls*

to look for" are big holes and waves, and they can be spotted from your boat. At moderate levels, chutes and drops appear. At low levels, the run becomes bony. In that case, climb out and scout The Last Drop which splits into two rocky Class 4 chutes — a long, steep, shallow cascade on the right and a short, jagged chute on the left. It has been run on both sides, but the left side is usually easier.

At extremely low levels The Last Drop becommes unrunnable, but taking out before this point is easy. When just past Double Whammy, you will recognize The Last Drop and the take-out by a large left-hand turn, a big pool, and steep steps up the left bank at Marie Canyon.

At all levels, the Cowichan is a fun run: short if you want it to be; longer if you want to play a lot. A manually operated gate in a weir at the outlet of Cowichan Lake opens to maintain minimum flow for fish and for the pulp mill at Duncan, but the effect is negligible for paddlers. Width averages 10 to 30 meters (30 to 100 feet) depending upon riverflow; the narrowest point is at the put-in. Gradient averages 7 meters/kilometer (35 feet/mile).

*Low water at S-Bend*

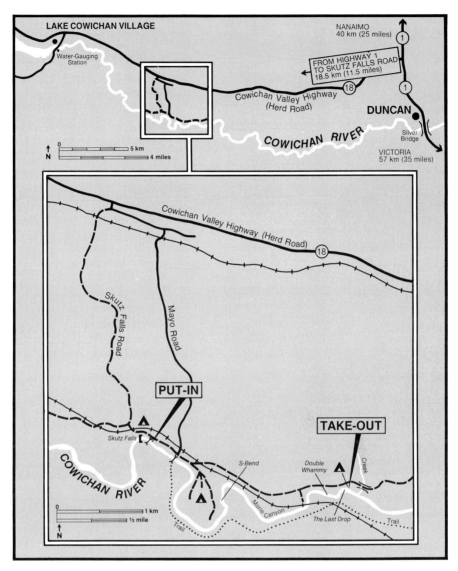

**Access to put-in and take-out:** Follow Trans-Canada Highway 1 (Island Highway) to Highway 18 (Herd Road) just north of Duncan. Head west on Highway 18 for 15 minutes to Skutz Falls Road. Turn left, cross railway tracks, and continue on gravel; just across another set of tracks, bear to the left and stop in the area near Skutz Falls; walk to a footbridge below the falls which is beside the put-in. Have a look and move on to the take-out.

Head downstream a short way to a fork: the narrow right-hand road leads to numerous secluded campsites beside the river; turn left, continuing along a wider gravel road across railway tracks and up a hill. Over the hill, when you see a bridge across a creek turn sharply right into the campsite at Marie Canyon. Steep wooden stairs to the take-out.

Return as you came and put in.

# CHEMAINUS RIVER
## *To Copper Canyon*

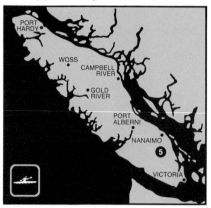

**Who:** Intermediate and advanced kayakers. No open-canoeists. No rafters

**Water to expect:** Class 2 and 3; one Class 4 drop. Some technical; mostly straightforward. Small volume

**Length of run:** 12.9 kilometers (8.0 miles); 2½ hours

**Shuttle one way:** 9.9 kilometers (6.2 miles); 15 minutes. Gravel logging road

**Season:** A "winter" river; October through April. Flashy; runnable after two or three days of rain. I kayaked it

**Why go:** Winter and it's cold? Want to play and be challenged but not for hour after hour?

This pretty paddle through wooded wilderness is both demanding and easy. Surfing waves and boils alternate with floaty sections, and the run climaxes at an exciting ledge-drop followed by a short intense blast between low, solid rock walls.

**Topographic Map:** 1:50,000 Duncan 92B/13.

**Facilities:** Camping, for a fee during peak season, at Ivy Green Provincial Park. It is 14.3 kilometers (8.9 miles) north of the flashing yellow light over Highway 1, past Ladysmith. A variety of private campgrounds along the highway, also for a fee — some with hot showers.

**Guidelines:** The run starts with surfing waves at the put-in. It soon goes through squirrelly water in a "box" canyon; just past your first sight of squared-off rock walls, then a boulder drop, you are into it. Paddlers who feel pushed by this first part can take out at Sally Creek. Beyond, a few more surfing waves and some Class 3 drops interspersed with long stretches of quiet water. At the end, a swiftly descending series of ledges before the river makes a sharp right turn, then a left; and all water funnels through a squiggly bend in the rock. This is Class 4. Most kayakers run the ledges on "river right". At the bottom of the ledges, climb from your boat to check that the final narrow dogleg through the rock is not blocked by a log or fallen tree. Shortly past the dogleg, the take-out pool.

The Chemainus averages 20 to 30 meters (70 to 100 feet) wide, and narrows to 3 meters (10 feet) in the final channel. Gradient averages 9 meters/kilometer (45 feet/mile). Recorded maximum riverflow: 457 m³/s (16,100 cfs) on January 19, 1968. It could happen again. A flash river! It rose ⅓ meter (1 foot) while we were on it. Rain throughout the night before, but no snow to melt, or the river would have risen even higher. There was enough

in mid-January with riverflow of 19 m$^3$/s (670 cfs); the name *Queen Mary* painted on concrete piers of the put-in bridge was "afloat"

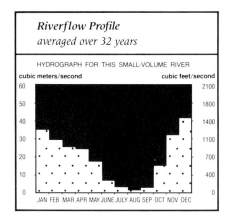

**Riverflow Profile**
*averaged over 32 years*

HYDROGRAPH FOR THIS SMALL-VOLUME RIVER

water for us to paddle; however we could have used more. And, if you put in and the river is too pushy, it is possible to climb out of this one. When kayaking the Chemainus, it feels like wilderness yet the road is never too far away.

*Surfing the Chemainus after rain*

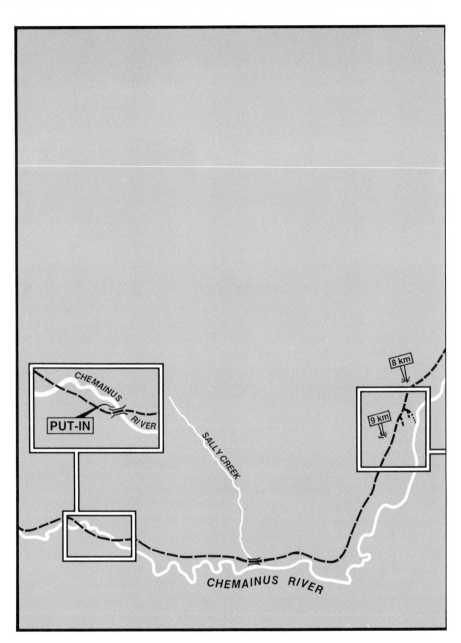

**Access to take-out and put-in:** From the flashing yellow light over Trans-Canada Highway 1 (Island Highway), head west on the logging road to a truck water tower on the left. When 2.7 kilometers (1.7 miles) past the tower, between the ''8 km'' and the ''9 km'' signs, turn left into an obscure pair of gravel tracks. A short way to a fork. Go left, then when the road becomes impassable, park. Walk about 400 paces down to the river and mark the take-out. Flag the side road too, where you turn onto the logging road, so you can easily return and find the take-out.

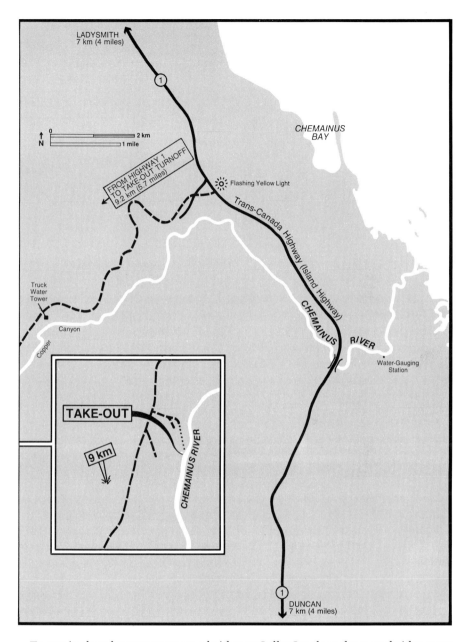

To put in, head upstream past a bridge at Sally Creek to the next bridge over the Chemainus.

---

This private industrial road usually is open to the public 24 hours a day, but drive cautiously. The best times to travel are on weekends, holidays, and weekdays after 5 p.m. However, logging trucks could still be on the road after that time. Always drive with your headlights on.

# NANAIMO RIVER
## M&B Bridge to White Rapids Mine

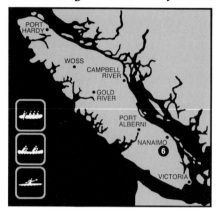

**Who:** Intermediate and advanced kayakers; guided novices. Expert open-canoeists and guided intermediates. Advanced and intermediate rafters

**Water to expect:** Class 2 and 3; at high levels, some Class 4. Medium volume. Rock gardens, technical ledges, shallow pools

**Length of run:** 11.9 kilometers (7.4 miles); 4 to 6 hours, depending on play time, for full run. From bridge to bridge is 7.3 kilometers (4.5 miles); 2 to 4 hours

**Why go:** Excellent short ledge-drops provide many places to play: hotdoggers are lured to the Nanaimo each spring for an annual April Fools' Day race.

Perfect also for those who just want to paddle in a beautiful place. Both the river and the countryside are untamed and lovely. Dark greenish-black water flows between low, newly forested hillsides; we noticed only one house. Roses bloom along the riverbanks. Rock walls resembling modern art forms surround you at the take-out. On shore you'll find coal from the abandoned mine; and the wild strawberries are sweet.

**Topographic Maps:** 1:50,000 Nanaimo Lakes 92F/1 and Nanaimo 92G/4.

**Facilities:** A pavilion, picnic tables, pit toilets, and lots of room to pitch tents provided free beside the outlet of the Nanaimo Lakes. Head upstream from the put-in: at a triple fork in the road past North Nanaimo River (Deadwood Creek) and before the gate, go left, cross railway tracks, turn right and go into the campground. Camping, for a fee during peak season, 14.9 kilometers (9.3 miles) beyond the take-out at Ivy Green Provincial Park. To reach this campground, go south on Highway 1 toward Ladysmith.

**Guidelines:** Optimum level for playing? Ideal when water has risen to ⅔ meter (2 feet) below the first step of the put-in bridge footings. If higher, it's pushy. When the foundation is under water, the Nanaimo is in flood with riverflow of at least 28 m³/s (1000 cfs).

Ledge play spots are scattered down the river: at low levels the run is ideal for novices but hard on boats. At medium levels it's perfect for playing. At high levels, watch out!

Some ledges are so straight across that they become "keepers" when the water is up. The Staircase, a series of ledges near the end of the run, can be sneaked on the left side of the right channel. All drops can be scouted from the water until the last one which is Class 4: a 3-meter (10-foot) high "house rock" sits in the middle of the passage; another on the right. You do not have

**Shuttle one way:** Full run: 10.8 kilometers (6.7 miles); 15 minutes. Bridge-to-bridge run: 6.4 kilometers (4 miles); 10 minutes. Gravel logging road for 1 kilometer (0.6 mile); mostly pavement

**Season:** Fall and spring are best, but runnable October through June. Principally rain-fed; also snow-melt. Moderated by lakes. I paddled it in early October with riverflow of 9 m$^3$/s (320 cfs)

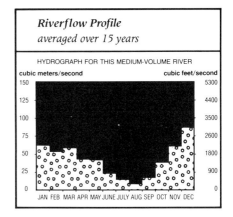

*Riverflow Profile*
*averaged over 15 years*

HYDROGRAPH FOR THIS MEDIUM-VOLUME RIVER

| cubic meters/second | | cubic feet/second |
|---|---|---|

to run the House Rock Drop; it is possible, and sometimes prudent, to pull out in the eddy on "river left" above it.

At high water, also check out whether you want to go 100 meters (330 feet) farther below the "house rock" between undercut walls to take out. If you are happy to paddle that part, you will find the take-out trail from the bottom of

*Water-carved walls at the take-out*

the canyon to where you are parked is an easier path to climb than the one on which you walked down to scout.

Width averages 6 to 30 meters (20 to 100 feet); the narrowest point is at the last drop. Gradient averages 7 meters/kilometer (35 feet/mile). Although riverflow is regulated by two dams above the run — at Fourth Lake and at Jump Creek — this seldom affects paddlers because usually releases are made to maintain flow in late summer when the river is too low to boat. Nevertheless, on one occasion kayakers were surprised to find the South Fork of the Nanaimo (which enters three drops past the put-in) in flood due to discharge from Jump Creek Dam. If this occurs, simply pull out on the left and walk back up the railway tracks — but listen for trains!

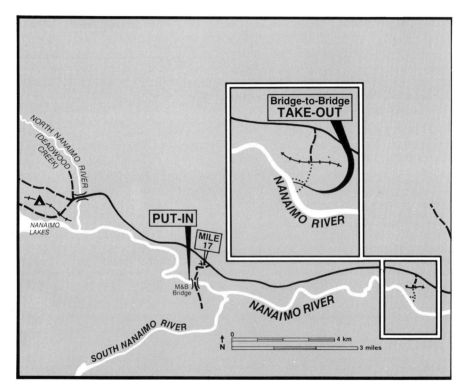

**Access to take-out and put-in:** Between Nanaimo and Ladysmith: from Trans-Canada Highway 1 (Island Highway), head up Nanaimo River Road; you will see signposts toward Nanaimo Lakes and Green Mountain. On going up the road, when 2.6 kilometers (1.6 miles) past where White Rapids Road enters, veer left onto a wide gravel roadway. Then turn left, cross railway tracks, and the way becomes very narrow. Drive down this rough gravel path to a large parking area beside dark gray heaps of mine tailings. From there, walk straight down a well-worn, steep rocky trail to the water: this takes 5 or 10 minutes. When you reach the river, you will find one take-out, which is useful at high water, slightly upstream. Then walk 200 paces downstream over beige sand and black sand and across rocks with smooth bowl shapes carved in them by the water, so you can see the last possible drop which is between the two 3-meter (10-foot) high "house rocks". Decide whether you want to take out before or after House Rock Drop.

A midway take-out: The bridge-to-bridge run is an alternative for those who want less run, more play time. To set up your take-out shuttle for it, continue up Nanaimo River Road. Small tracks lead off all along, so carefully note directions and distance. Shortly past where a gravel road enters on the right, Nanaimo River Road crosses a gorge; concrete guardrails line the route. When 0.5 kilometer (0.3 mile) beyond them, turn left into a narrow gravel path. Go to railway tracks and park. Walk downhill along the washed-out roadway which switches back to the right to see the take-out; at a split in the roadway,

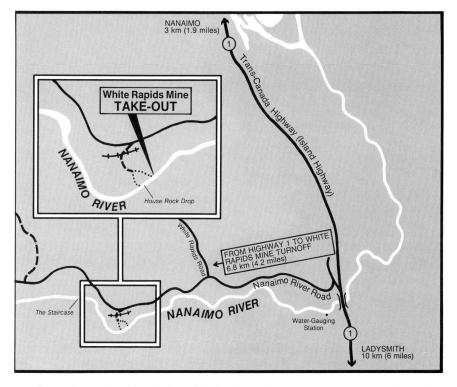

continue along the right fork which is the easiest way to the water. From the railway tracks, it's only 5 or 10 minutes to the remains of an old bridge.

To put in for either the full run to White Rapids Mine or the shorter bridge-to-bridge run, continue upstream on Nanaimo River Road to a MacMillan Bloedel sign at Mile 17; then go left down a curving gravel logging road to the bridge.

---

This private industrial road is open to the public as far as the bridge, but go cautiously because logging trucks might be hauling on it. Drive with your headlights on.

# WICKANINNISH BEACH
## *Ocean Surf*

**Who:** All kayakers on 1-meter (3-foot) high waves; intermediate and advanced kayakers with Eskimo roll on larger ones. Expert open-canoeists on waves up to 1 meter (3 feet) high. No rafters

**Water to expect:** Varies from flat water, which is rare, up to 5-meter (16-foot) high waves. Almost always at least ½-meter (1½-foot) high surf. A gently shelving sandy beach

**Length of run:** Depending on wave height, the surf breaks from 300 meters (1000 feet) offshore into the beach and the point

**Why go:** Of all mid-island surf sites, the highest waves are usually at Wickaninnish.

And what's in the name? In the book titled *1001 British Columbia Place Names* by G.P.V. and Helen B. Akrigg, there is an account of dealings with Chief Wicananish back in 1788. More about "the Wickaninnish, a large and powerful tribe" in 1803: It is said that they carved their canoes with greater skill than that of the other tribes and used sails as well as paddles. Wind is still a big consideration at this site which is exposed to an unobstructed sweep from the open Pacific.

**Tide Tables:** *Canadian Tide & Current Tables, Volume 6, Barkley Sound and Discovery Passage to Dixon Entrance*; refer to Tofino daily tables. When you reach the coast, stop and obtain a free map of the park, tide tables, and news of weather from the park information center.

**Facilities:** An outdoor tap where you can wash gear with fresh water and a restroom with flush toilets are beside the parking lot and beach. "The Wick" restaurant, with a view of the surf, is immediately southeast of beach parking and is open different hours in different seasons. Telephone (604)726-7151 to check on it. Camping, for a fee during peak season, at the first-come, first-served campground at Green Point high above Long Beach; open year-round but very crowded in summer. Picnic tables, flush toilets, and fire rings are provided. Camping (also for a fee during peak season, but the fee is less than that at Green Point) is more often available at Schooner walk-in campground at the northwestern end of Long Beach, and is reached by a 1¼-kilometer (¾-mile) trail. Fresh water and pit toilets are provided at these sites; fires permitted below high tide. Or, in summer, reserve space and enjoy hot showers at privately owned Pacific Rim Campground (usually open from April to October) just north of the park boundary at Cox Bay.

**Guidelines:** Offshore wind from the southeast improves the surf; no wind is also good. Onshore wind ruins it; sideshore wind is tolerable unless it is high

**Shuttle one way:** None required

**Season:** Year-round. Highest waves in winter when stormy out at sea. We kayak-surfed it in mid-July on an incoming tide with 1½-meter (5-foot) high waves

*Down to the surf in summer*

velocity. West wind prevails but it rarely blows before noon, so usually the best time to surf is in the morning. Remember also that surf is highest on an incoming tide. There are rocks at the southeastern end of the Wickaninnish "break" and in summer the prevailing riptide is toward them; so be sure to watch where you are drifting. It helps to have a good Eskimo roll, especially when waves are big.

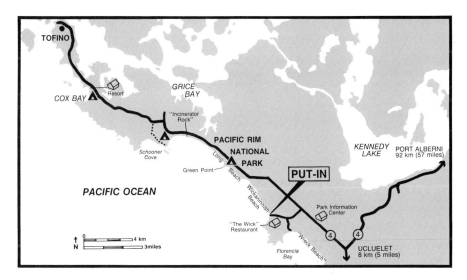

**Access to the put-in:** Located in Pacific Rim National Park on the West Coast. From Nanaimo a 2½-hour drive by way of Port Alberni to Wickaninnish Beach. As you head west on Highway 4, at the junction with the road to Ucluelet turn right toward Tofino. Pass the park information center then turn left off the highway toward Wickaninnish. Go 2.9 kilometers (1.8 miles) and turn right to beach parking. It's a short walk to the beach put-in.

# LONG BEACH
## *Ocean Surf*

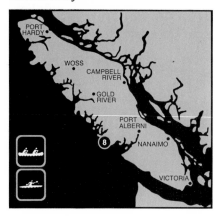

**Who:** All kayakers on 1-meter (3-foot) high waves; intermediate and advanced kayakers with Eskimo roll on larger ones. Expert open-canoeists on waves up to 1 meter (3 feet) high. No rafters

**Water to expect:** Varies from flat up to 4-meter (13-foot) high waves, well spaced. Rarely flat; almost always surfable at this very gently shelving sandy beach

**Length of run:** Depending on wave height, surf breaks from 200 meters (700 feet) offshore into the beach

**Shuttle one way:** None required

**Why go:** This is where the "clean break" happens most often. With few obstructions to chop up the surf, and waves well spaced, four breaks at a time, it's good for experienced surfers. Excellent for a big group that is learning: the smooth break, regular intervals between waves, and sand to wash up onto at this broad beach make it easy. During summer, surf guards are nearby.

Long Beach stretches for 11 kilometers (7 miles). A variety of campgrounds are in the area; some nearby motel accommodations; and almost always surf.

**Tide Tables:** *Canadian Tide & Current Tables, Volume 6, Barkley Sound and Discovery Passage to Dixon Entrance*; refer to Tofino daily tables. When you reach the coast, stop and obtain a free map of the park, tide tables, and news of weather from the park information center.

**Facilities:** Two parking areas at the northwest end of Long Beach, each providing restrooms with flush toilets and outdoor taps where you can rinse gear with fresh water.

Camping at first-come, first-served campground at Green Point high above Long Beach; open year-round but very crowded in summer. Picnic tables, flush toilets, and fire rings provided. Camping is more often available at Schooner walk-in campground at the northwestern end of Long Beach, reached by a 1¼-kilometer (¾-mile) trail. Fresh water and pit toilets provided; fires permitted below high tide line. During peak season a fee is charged at both of these national park sites. Just north of park boundary at Cox Bay, camping space can be reserved and there are hot showers at privately owned Pacific Rim Campground; however, it is normally open only from Easter to October.

**Guidelines:** In winter when it is stormy out at sea, the surf builds to huge proportions, up to a height of 5 meters (16 feet). Surf championships, sponsored by a kayak club from Nanaimo, are held at Long Beach in October. Summer is the time to learn, yet many holidayers use the area then, and

**Season:** Year-round. Wave height varies daily: up to 4 meters (13 feet) high in winter; 2 meters (6 feet) in summer. I kayak-surfed it in early July and late August on an incoming tide with ½- and 1-meter (1½- and 3-foot) high waves

*Surf kayak*

*Beachcombers, swimmers, boaters*

*Place to learn: a small "clean break"*

boaters must be careful not to hit swimmers. A broached kayak is uncontrollable: therefore kayakers should avoid areas where there are board-surfers and swimmers, particularly small children. Also remember that it is much much easier to catch a wave in a kayak than on a surf board, and make an effort to share the waves fairly with board riders.

When many people are present, the preferred area for boaters is the surf southeast of the spot that some locals refer to as "Incinerator Rock", which is near the northernmost parking lot.

More points: the surfer nearest the "curl" (breaking part of the wave) has the right of way and others should not take off on the same wave. Avoid low-tide waves which become "dumpers" in shallow water; the surf is best on an incoming tide. Sometimes there are dangerous riptides around the major offshore rock; it varies with the season. When at Long Beach, ask surf guards which area is best that day.

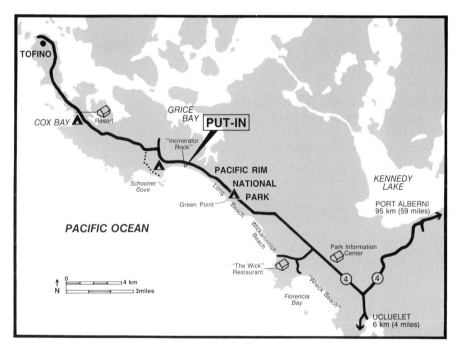

**Access to put-in:** Located in Pacific Rim National Park on the West Coast. From Nanaimo a 2½-hour drive by way of Port Alberni. As you head west on Highway 4, at the junction with the road to Ucluelet turn right toward Tofino; pass the park information center. From there, it is 13.5 kilometers (8.4 miles) more on the highway, passing turnoffs to Wickaninnish, Green Point, and a couple of parking lots for Long Beach, to the northernmost lot. This is the smallest parking area, but it is closest to the surf. Climb over drifted logs or follow one of the trails — only a few steps to the beach.

If the small parking lot is full, return to the larger one and walk down one of several short trails to the sand and put in.

# COX BAY
## *Ocean Surf*

**Who:** All kayakers on 1-meter (3-foot) high waves; intermediate and advanced kayakers with Eskimo roll on larger ones. Expert open-canoeists on waves up to 1 meter (3 feet) high. No rafters

**Water to expect:** Varies from flat up to 5-meter (16-foot) high waves. Rarely flat; almost always at least ½-meter (1½-foot) high surf. Waves come in quick succession at this gently shelving sandy beach

**Length of run:** Depending on wave height, the surf breaks from 400 meters

**Why go:** Big surf — when it's good. But what really makes this site different from others is the facilities. Kayak-surf and enjoy a hot shower afterward at your campground or housekeeping cabin: both are available, both can be reserved. The campground is open from Easter to October; the beachfront resort year-round. With a hot shower to return to, what a pleasure to surf in stormy weather in winter!

**Tide Tables:** *Canadian Tide & Current Tables, Volume 6, Barkley Sound and Discovery Passage to Dixon Entrance*; refer to Tofino daily tables. A good map of the area and tide tables are available free at the national park information center.

**Facilities:** Camping for a fee at privately owned Pacific Rim Campground which offers a variety of services: coin-operated hot showers, laundromat, trailer hookups, a fast-seafood concession, a small grocery. When reserving an individual or group campsite, consider proximity to the beach: three paths of varying lengths lead to it from different parts of the campground. It can take from 1 to 30 minutes to reach the surf, depending on the location of your campsite within the area. Ask for one close to the beach. Contact Pacific Rim Campground Resorts, P.O. Box 570, Tofino, B.C. V0R 2Z0, telephone (604)725-3202.

Housekeeping cabins, some with fireplaces, suites with fireplaces and full kitchens, and sleeping rooms are available at Pacific Sands Resort, P.O. Box 237, Tofino, B.C. V0R 2Z0, telephone (604)725-3322.

**Guidelines:** The best place to surf at Cox Bay is at the center of the beach away from rocks at the north end. Two islands offshore either protect this bay or create cross waves, depending on wind direction; the surf is biggest when there is a southeast wind. It can be rough, difficult surf with high frequency. Sometimes the waves just keep coming one after another in quick succession, up to 12 in a row. On those days, necessary to have a good Eskimo roll. Best on

(1300 feet) offshore into the beach

**Shuttle one way:** None required

**Season:** Year-round. The best season
depends on your confidence level;
highest waves in winter when stormy
out at sea. I kayak-surfed it in mid-July
on incoming and outgoing tides, and
in late August on an incoming tide with
waves 1, 1½, and 2 meters (3, 5, and
6 feet) high

*Winter and summer, "ender country"*

an incoming tide. Surfing conditions vary daily: if they don't look good where
you are, check out other nearby locations.

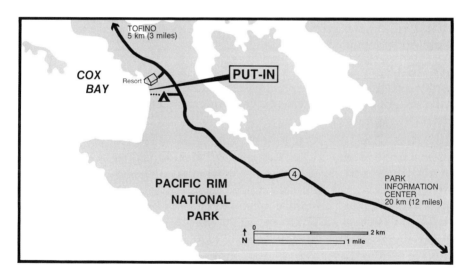

**Access to put-in:** Located near Tofino on the West Coast. From Nanaimo, a
2½-hour drive by way of Port Alberni to the information center at Pacific Rim
National Park. Then continue north through the park passing turnoffs to
Wickaninnish Beach, Green Point, Long Beach, and Grice Bay. When
2.3 kilometers (1.4 miles) past the park boundary, go left into Pacific Rim
Campground; from there, a 1-minute walk along a trail to the beach, or a
short way beyond the road to the campground, turn into Pacific Sands Resort
which is on the beach.

Parking space and a short public access trail to the beach are near the campground amphitheater.

# CAMPBELL RIVER
*Power Plant to Logging Bridge*

**Who:** Novice kayakers; guided novice and intermediate open-canoeists; rafters

**Water to expect:** Class 2—. Medium volume, and swift but not complex

**Length of run:** 1.9 kilometers (1.2 miles); 1 hour

**Shuttle one way:** 1.7 kilometers (1.1 miles); 5 minutes. Paved highway

**Season:** Year-round. Rain-fed and snow-melt. Dam-controlled but continuously flowing; occasional large releases. I paddled it in late July;

**Why go:** Short and straightforward — a good training stretch for beginners: fairly fast water; few rocks; almost no sweepers. Suitable for practicing ferrying across the river, for pointing out the danger of bridge piers, and for playing on uncomplicated rapids.

Paddling all year: when rivers have dried up everywhere else, there is still water in the Campbell.

**Topographic Map:** 1:50,000 Quadra Island 92K/3.

**Facilities:** Camping midway in the shuttle route across the highway from the river. Picnic tables, pit toilets, and fire rings provided, for a fee during peak season, at Elk Falls Provincial Park.

**Guidelines:** The best rapids are at the start near the power plant. From there the gradient is steady, averaging 8 meters/kilometer (40 feet/mile); and the river is a 75-meter (250-foot) wide expanse of riffled water with a few holes. From beginning to end of this run the Campbell is continuously flowing; there are few pools. Rescue is not easy. Also watch for Whale Rock near midstream just past where Quinsam River flows in on the right, three-fourths of the way along the run. Past it, when nearing the take-out bridge, move quickly to the right and stay clear of the bridge piers so that you do not wrap your boat around one.

The Campbell River has been dam-controlled during the entire period in which riverflow records have been kept. Therefore the hydrograph above reflects the pattern of flow that you can expect. Since the river is controlled to create hydroelectric power, riverflow is reasonably consistent all year. The average flow along this stretch is 99 m³/s (3500 cfs) You will probably find it at about that level; however, on November 15, 1953, there was a maximum recorded riverflow of 835 m³/s (29,500 cfs) .A sign at the take-out warns: "River level is subject to sudden rises". When a siren sounds near the Quinsam River indicating that there will be a release from the dam, you have 10 minutes to get off of — or onto — the river.

precise riverflow data unavailable; my
guess is 90 m³/s (3180 cfs)

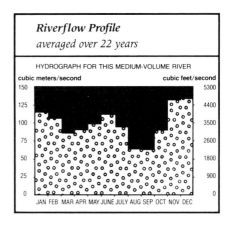

After paddling, you may want to go to Elk Falls Provincial Park to walk or
drive across the John Hart Dam. Below it, walk along wooded trails to Moose,
Deer, and Elk Falls.

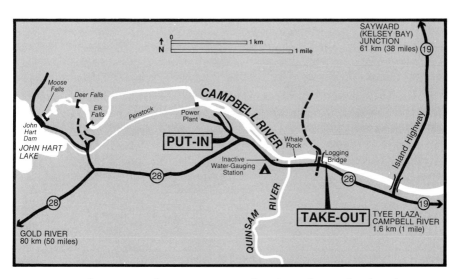

**Access to take-out and put-in:** As you head north on Island Highway 19,
pass Tyee Plaza in the town of Campbell River; on the way out of town where
Island Highway turns right and crosses the river, you go straight on Highway 28 following signs to Gold River. Go 1.0 kilometer (0.6 mile), turn right
and leave your shuttle vehicle beside the take-out bridge. Park well off the
road because logging trucks might be hauling over it.

To put in, continue upstream on Highway 28 for 1.1 kilometers (0.7 mile)
to a road that veers right. Go along it through the gate with a signpost advising
that it closes at 4 p.m, and put in below the power plant.

# WHITE RIVER
## *Waterfall to First Bridge*

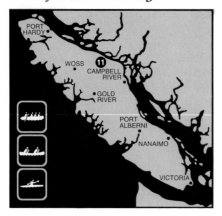

**Who:** Intermediate and advanced kayakers; no open-canoeists; intermediate and advanced rafters. At lower levels, also guided novice kayakers; expert open-canoeists; guided novice rafters

**Water to expect:** Class 2 through 3+. At high levels, Class 4 in the canyon. Small volume; both technical water and straightforward water

**Length of run:** 16.0 kilometers (9.9 miles); 4 hours

**Shuttle one way:** 11.6 kilometers (7.2 miles); 15 minutes. Restricted

**Why go:** A waterfall to view, surfing waves, and technical drops. Kayakers graduating from Class 2 to 3 will find it a good transitional river. You can pick and choose. Except in the canyon at the height of runoff, it is easy to portage all drops. An excellent river to paddle with a mixed group. It's fun and manageable for those with a variety of skills.

You will experience a wilderness feeling while on the White River even though the area is being logged and the road is never far away. We saw two deer while setting up shuttle.

**Topographic Maps:** 1:50,000 Brewster Lake 92K/4 and Sayward 92K/5.

**Facilities:** Picnic tables, pit toilets, and fire rings are free at the campground beside Elk Creek; to reach it, immediately after turning off Island Highway turn right into Orecan Road. Camping, for a fee, at White River Court where there are hot showers.

**Guidelines:** The waterfall looked dangerous to me during runoff in late May. I do not recommend running it at any level, but others do. We put in on the pool below the falls and found lots of good water downstream: Class 2 to 3+. Surfing waves up to 1 meter (3 feet) high; then drops and pools through a constricted canyon. The river broadens, and the last part is an easy Class 2 float. Its width ranges from 10 to 45 meters (30 to 150 feet). Overall gradient averages 9 meters/kilometer (45 feet/mile); but in the canyon it is 24 meters/ kilometer (125 feet/mile) — though it did not seem that great.

At the end of May few rocks and boulders were showing, except in the canyon. Evergreens and shrubs grow close to the banks. Watch for sweepers and fallen trees. Although we did not see wood in the river during the run, we saw logs beside it at the put-in. The area is surrounded with logging operations; so keep a sharp lookout for semi-submerged cables, and for other logging trash that has been seen in the river.

gravel logging road

**Season:** October through July; best in May and June. Rain-fed and snow-melt. We paddled it in late May; precise riverflow data unavailable; my guess is 30 m³/s (1060 cfs)

*Kayakers at the put-in*

*Lunch in the sun*

*Crepes suzettes beside campfire*

White River Road is restricted: travel usually is permitted on weekends, holidays, and weekdays before 7 a.m. and after 5 p.m. However, logging trucks could still be hauling after that time. When possible, follow a radio-controlled vehicle. Always drive with your headlights on. If you want to use this private industrial road during working hours it may be possible. To check on this and to obtain current information on possible fire-hazard closures, contact MacMillan Bloedel, Sayward, B.C. V0P 1R0, telephone (604)282-3331.

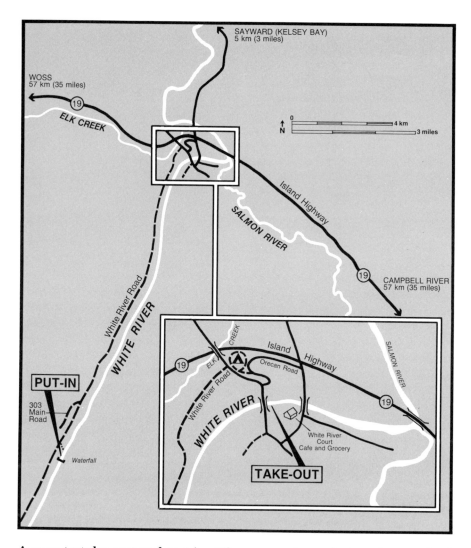

**Access to take-out and put-in:** When you arrive at the junction on Island Highway 19 where a sign points to Sayward and Kelsey Bay, turn off the highway in the opposite direction. Pass Orecan Road and a resort, cross a bridge, pass White River Court. Turn right, then right again, and go to the next bridge over the White: the take-out.

For the put-in, continue a short way to White River Road; turn left and go up it 10.4 kilometers (6.5 miles). Measure the distance: when 0.7 kilometer (0.4 mile) past where 303 Main Road veers off, park on the left at the roadside in a lay-by with the signpost "Trail to Base of Waterfall". Follow a rough trail through the trees to the river, and see the waterfall on your right. A difficult approach: there just is no easy way down this steep bank covered with raspberry and huckleberry bushes. However, there is a good eddy at the base of the clump of trees; make your way down the bank and put in below the waterfall.

# ADAM RIVER
## *To Rooney Lake Junction*

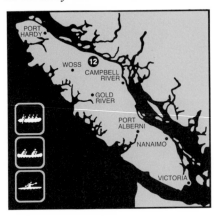

**Who:** All kayakers; intermediate and expert open-canoeists; paddle rafters

**Water to expect:** Class 2. Low volume; a steady gradient with riffles and a couple of drops

**Length of run:** 4.3 kilometers (2.7 miles); 1 hour

**Shuttle one way:** 4.2 kilometers (2.6 miles); 10 minutes. Gravel logging roads

**Season:** October through June; best in May and June. Rain-fed and snow-melt; a flash stream. I paddled it in late May; precise riverflow data unavailable; my guess is 17 m³/s (600 cfs)

**Why go:** A short, fun evening run. Play waves at a couple of drops. Short rock gardens too in this mostly gravel-bottomed part of the stream that flows through a broad, recently logged valley. A corridor of trees lines the river, makes it feel wild. Little creeks trickle in. The water is a strange rusty color. I found a hole to play in that dumped me a couple of times. Paddlers with me dubbed it "Betty's Surprise".

**Topographic Map:** 1:50,000 Adam River 92L/8.

**Facilities:** Camping is free in the large undeveloped wooded area at the take-out for the canyon run with "Fishing Parking" signpost.

**Guidelines:** The gradient averages 7 meters/kilometer (35 feet/mile). Width varies from 3 to 30 meters (10 to 100 feet). Play waves are up to 1 meter (3 feet) high. Riverflow increases quickly on the Adam because there is no forest cover to hold the rain in this newly logged valley: a very flashy stream. The mountains are high and runoff comes later to these mid-island sites than to rivers on the east or west coast. Watch for sweepers. Do not miss the take-out bridge or you will be into the canyon.

**Access to put-in and take-out:** The put-in is beside Island Highway 19 bridge over the Adam. To reach the take-out, turn north off Highway 19 into a gravel logging road immediately west of the bridge. Go downhill and take the right fork. Head downstream to the bridge at Rooney Lake Junction. Leave a shuttle vehicle at the take-out.

Return to Highway 19 and put in.

---

These logging roads may be restricted: travel usually is permitted 24 hours a day; however, there might be logging traffic too. Always drive with your headlights on. Observe the following signposts at road entries:

Red: Active logging area that is open to the public only on weekends, holidays, and weekdays before 7 a.m. and after 5 p.m.

Yellow: Open to the public but also used by heavy vehicles. Drive with extreme caution and always yield to logging traffic.

Green: Open to the public except during fire-hazard closures.

To learn about possible closures, and to inform drivers of radio-controlled vehicles to watch for you on these private industrial roads, contact MacMillan Bloedel, Sayward, B.C. V0P 1R0, telephone (604)282-3331.

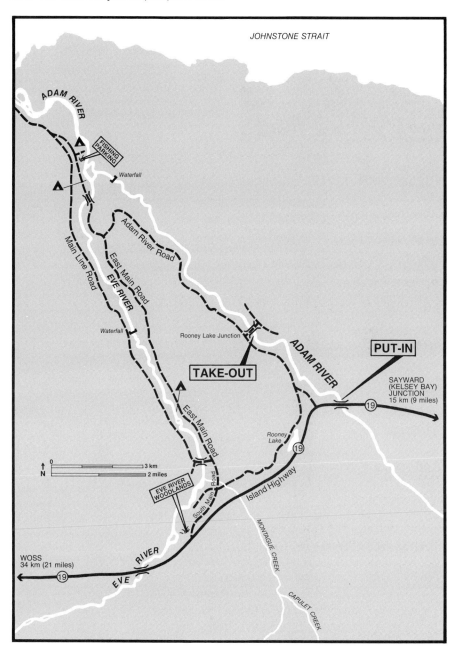

# ADAM RIVER
## *The Canyon*

**Who:** Advanced kayakers and guided intermediates; no open-canoeists; no rafters

**Water to expect:** Class 3 to 4+, and three mandatory portages (two short, one an hour long) in a remote canyon. Unrunnable at high levels. Drops and pools; technical

**Length of run:** 9.7 kilometers (6.0 miles); 4 hours, including portages

**Shuttle one way:** 10.8 kilometers (6.7 miles); 15 minutes. Gravel logging roads

**Why go:** Adam to Eve — ultimate beginnings? Primeval wilderness? The Adam River offers challenging drops and pools through an intimate and splendrous canyon.

**Topographic Map:** 1:50,000 Adam River 92L/8.

**Facilities:** Camping is free at the large, undeveloped wooded area at the take-out; the turnoff is marked with the signpost "Fishing Parking".

**Guidelines:** The surrounding countryside is raw from recent logging, but this soon becomes unnoticeable to the kayaker. A corridor of trees remains; between them is an extremely narrow canyon. Proceed with caution. Almost immediately after putting in, we encountered a large tree fallen across the river. We were able to duck it, but at slightly higher water level this would not be possible.

Past the tree, there are about 20 steep technical drops, two being Class 6 (both easy to carry your kayaks around). We never did see one of them (thus a mandatory portage), and later the logging company engineer told me a 60-meter (200-foot) waterfall is in that gorge. The rest of the run up to it is Class 3 to 4+. Scout carefully as you go. A large rock is in the middle of the last runnable drop. Shortly past that split chute it is impossible to see around the corner; when we paddled it, a tree was across the entrance to the gorge with the waterfall in it. A high, sheer wall rises on the left; another almost as high on the right. The 1-hour portage begins here: climb up either bank. If you are carrying around on the left bank, bushwhack over the backbone of the hill, then down to the right and put in on slow-moving braided water. If carrying around on the right bank, put in when you see calm water. Just past the confluence with the Eve River, look for your take-out marker.

The Adam is narrow. It starts at a width of 20 meters (70 feet) and constricts to a width of 2 meters (6 feet) at some drops, then broadens to 30 or 40 meters (100 or 130 feet) upon merging with the Eve. The overall gradient averages

**Season:** Fall and spring; best in May and June. Snow-melt and rain-fed; extremely flashy. I paddled it in late May; precise riverflow data unavailable; my guess is 17 m³/s (600 cfs)

*Studying the topographic map*

only 14 meters/kilometer (75 feet/mile), and much of the drop is at the end where three contours crowd the last couple of kilometers indicating the waterfall. Throughout the rest of the run, boulders combine with radical narrowing to create the not-too-pushy (at least when we paddled it) but always interesting water in this beautiful canyon. Magnificent kayaking at

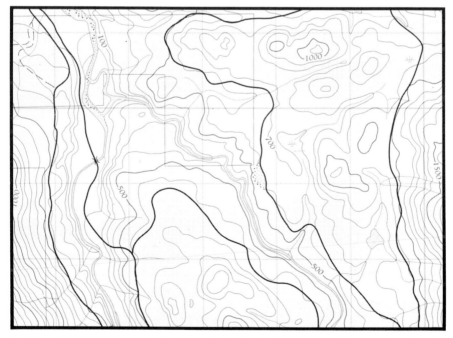

Portion of 1:50,000 topographic map Adam River 92L/8. Waterfall not marked on it; for location of waterfall, see access map next page. Refer also to pages 23 and 112 for information on obtaining and using "topo" maps.

moderate levels, but at high water levels it is dangerous and unrunnable. Having practically no forest cover to delay runoff, this river is extremely flashy.

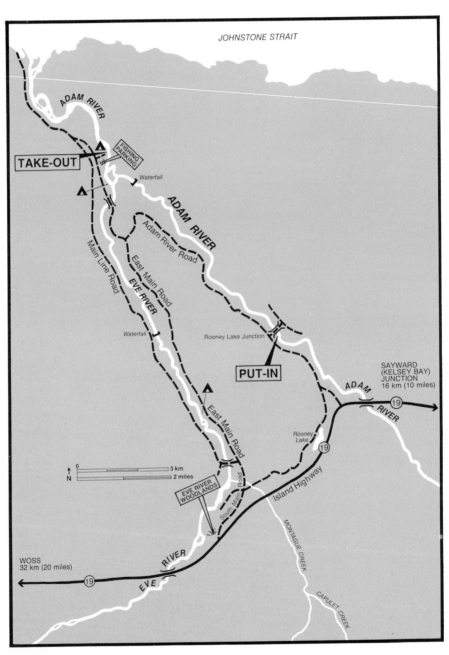

**Access to put-in and take-out:** From Island Highway 19 immediately west of a bridge over the Adam, turn north into a gravel logging road, go downhill and take the right fork. Head downstream to the bridge at Rooney Lake Junction which is your put-in. Take a look and then continue downstream to place your shuttle vehicle.

Shortly after the road leaves the river it bends left down a hill. When you reach a fork, keep right and continue downhill to a bridge over the Eve River. Then go 1.6 kilometers (1.0 mile) past that bridge to a side road on the right with the signpost "Fishing Parking". Drive to the end of it, walk 60 paces through the woods, and mark your take-out.

Return as you came to Rooney Lake Junction and put in.

---

These logging roads may be restricted: travel usually is permitted 24 hours a day; however, there could be logging traffic too. Always drive with your headlights on. Observe the signposts:

Red: Active logging area that is open to the public only on weekends, holidays, and weekdays before 7 a.m. and after 5 p.m.

Yellow: Open to the public but also used by heavy vehicles. Drive with extreme caution and always yield to logging traffic.

Green: Open to the public except during fire-hazard closures.

To learn about possible closures, and to inform drivers of radio-controlled vehicles to watch for you on these private industrial roads, contact MacMillan Bloedel, Sayward, B.C. V0P 1R0, telephone (604)282-3331.

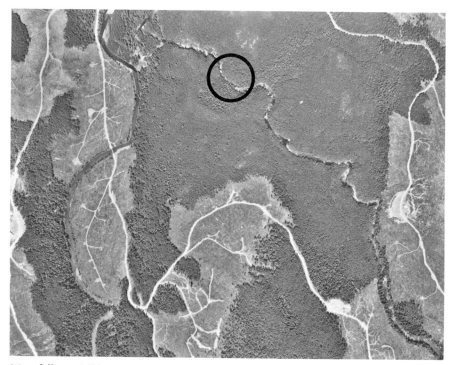

*Waterfall not visible on air photo of Adam River*

# EVE RIVER
## *Montague Creek to Lower Bridge*

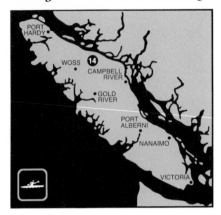

**Who:** Intermediate and advanced kayakers; no open-canoeists; no rafters

**Water to expect:** Class 2 and 3+; a Class 4 drop and a Class 5 or 6 waterfall (portageable). Steady gradient most of the way; some technical

**Length of run:** 10.9 kilometers (6.8 miles); 3½ hours

**Shuttle one way:** 9.6 kilometers (6.0 miles); 15 minutes. Gravel logging roads

**Season:** Fall and spring; best in May or June. Rain-fed and snow-melt. When

**Why go:** One good reason is if you like small rivers. This stream has a fairly constant descent, much of it over gravel, with one excellent boulder-strewn cascade. The Eve's pale-green waters flow through a fern-clad valley scarred with tree stumps. She's ugly — she's beautiful!

**Topographic Map:** 1:50,000 Adam River 92L/8.

**Facilities:** Camping is free at two small sites beside the Eve, and at a large, undeveloped wooded area below the confluence with the Adam River.

**Guidelines:** Small, shallow, and dangerous, as well as beautiful, the Eve is most safely runnable during spring peak. The highest water is in the fall, but the greatest amount of debris is in the river then; thus spring runoff is the best time. Sources of the Eve are Kunnum, Montague, and Capulet Creeks arising on Jagged Mountain, Mount Romeo, and Mount Juliet. High mountains, all exceeding 1600 meters (5200 feet), therefore her spring peak is slightly later than most rivers on Vancouver Island.

Gradient averages 12 meters/kilometer (65 feet/mile). Although the river is not too pushy, the danger from fallen trees, sweepers, and logjams is magnified because logging operations are on all sides and because the Eve is narrow. From 15 meters (50 feet) wide at the start, the banks of the Eve spread to 30 meters (100 feet) at the take-out. Eddy-hop in control all the way: you may have to carry around fallen trees or logs. When halfway through the run, look for an excellent bouldery stretch leading into the triple cascade waterfall. When you cannot see around a corner to the right, it is time to portage. Climb up and over the right bank which is short and steep. This takes 10 minutes. We stopped for lunch on the other side.

the gravel at the take-out is just covered with water the Eve is optimum level. We paddled it in late May; precise riverflow data unavailable; my guess is 11 m³/s (390 cfs)

*In a fern-clad valley*

*Eddy-hopping*

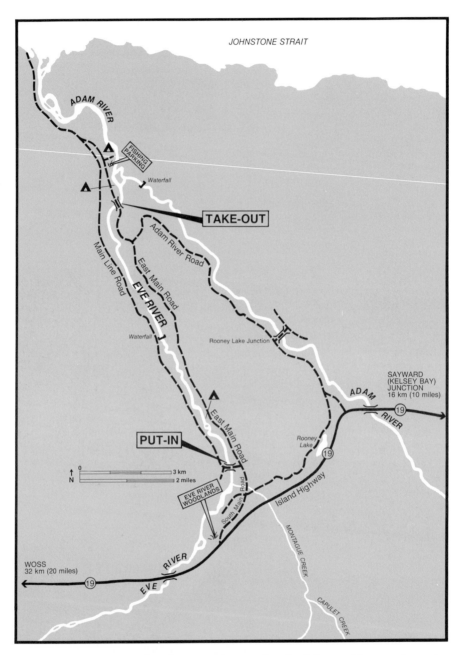

JOHNSTONE STRAIT

ADAM RIVER

FISHING
PARKING

Waterfall

TAKE-OUT

Adam River Road

East Main Road

Main Line Road

EVE RIVER

Waterfall

Rooney Lake Junction

SAYWARD
(KELSEY BAY)
JUNCTION
16 km (10 miles)

ADAM

RIVER

19

PUT-IN

East Main Road

Rooney
Lake

19

0        3 km
N        2 miles

EVE RIVER
WOODLANDS

South Main Road

Island Highway

MONTAGUE CREEK

WOSS
32 km (20 miles)

19

EVE

RIVER

CAPULET CREEK

**Access to put-in and take-out:** From Island Highway 19, turn into the road with a signpost "Eve River Woodlands"; this road is between the Adam and Eve Rivers. Go along it 1.9 kilometers (1.2 miles) to a triple fork in the road: keep to the center fork for 1 kilometer (0.6 mile), then turn left and stop to take a look at the put-in bridge.

To reach the take-out, return to the road you came along and continue downstream along East Main Road. Where Adam River Road enters from the right, stay left and continue downhill to the take-out bridge over the Eve. Head back upstream and put in.

---

Eve River woodlands roads may be restricted: travel usually is permitted 24 hours a day; however, logging trucks might be on them too. Always drive with your headlights on. Observe the signposts:

Red: Active logging area that is open to the public only on weekends, holidays, and weekdays before 7 a.m. and after 5 p.m.

Yellow: Open to the public but also used by heavy vehicles. Drive with extreme caution and always yield to logging traffic.

Green: Open to the public except during fire-hazard closures.

To learn about possible closures, and to inform drivers of radio-controlled vehicles to watch for you on these private industrial roads, contact MacMillan Bloedel, Sayward, B.C. V0P 1R0, telephone (604)282-3353 or 287-7473.

*Boulder stretch*

# DAVIE-NIMPKISH RIVERS
*Island Highway to Woss*

**Who:** Advanced kayakers and guided intermediates; no open-canoeists; no rafters

**Water to expect:** Class 2+ to 3+; two Class 4 drops and a Class 4 or 5 waterfall or fish ladder (all portageable). Small volume to medium volume; continuous rock garden, then steep drops and pools

**Length of run:** 14.0 kilometers (8.7 miles); 4 hours

**Shuttle one way:** 12.2 kilometers (7.6 miles); 15 minutes. Paved highway

**Why go:** Railway Drop — plus another not-quite-so-hard big, steep drop before the wrecked bridge; a cascade; a waterfall — and miles of continuous rock garden. You probably will not stop to play on the Davie because there is so much maneuvering, then excitement, just running it.

Tired of dust? An incredibly easy paved shuttle sets you up for these dramatic watery "stairsteps" through the wilds.

**Topographic Maps:** 1:50,000 Schoen Lake 92L/1 and Woss Lake 92L/2.

**Facilities:** Picnic tables, pit toilets, and fire rings provided free at campgrounds beside the Klaklakama Lakes and Woss Lake.

**Guidelines:** Continuous Class 2 and 3 rock gardens demand constant attention. Many sweepers and fallen trees too. We came across one newly fallen tree, still with all of its branches, blocking the stream: the worst kind of "strainer". Two-thirds of the way down the Davie the rock gardens become more difficult. The river bends left, and there is a steep Class 3+ drop — worth scouting. We call that last one Wrecked Bridge Drop, because just past it remnants of a railway bridge are scattered in the bush on shore. Soon the river bends left again and a trestle spans Railway Drop: beneath it, a steep Class 4 cascade cushions off of a head wall, curls around the corner, and bounces down a steep channel into standing waves at the bottom. Stop to scout.

Shortly downstream, climb from your boat again to scout the final Class 4 "stairstep" cascade into the Nimpkish (Kla-anch). At low water, it is unrunnable. From here on, Class 2 and 3 with lots of water to the broad 2- to 3-meter (6- to 10-foot) high waterfall just before the bridge, or a narrow fish ladder to run. Or you can take out at a big eddy above them. The Class 4 to 5 falls are split with rocks in the middle. We ran it on "river left" down a sloping green tongue. Two years before, when the water level was lower, I carried around it. Volume varies the "keeper" at the bottom; the danger changes from day to day, so judgment is required.

**Season:** Spring runoff and fall; best in late May to mid-June, when I paddled it; precise riverflow data unavailable; my guess is 25 m$^3$/s (880 cfs)

*Playing at Davie River put-in*

The Davie is 30 meters (100 feet) wide at the put-in, and averages 40-meter (130-foot) width to the Nimpkish confluence; then it broadens to 80 meters (260 feet). The gradient averages 8 meters/kilometer (40 feet/mile). The first two-thirds of the Davie descends at a steady rate; the last third is like stairsteps; and once you are on the Nimpkish, the run flattens until you reach the falls. The take-out is a steep climb: look for a trail on the right bank above the fish ladder around the falls.

*Waterfall on Nimpkish River at take-out*

*Fish ladder on Nimpkish River*

*Drops and pools on Davie River*

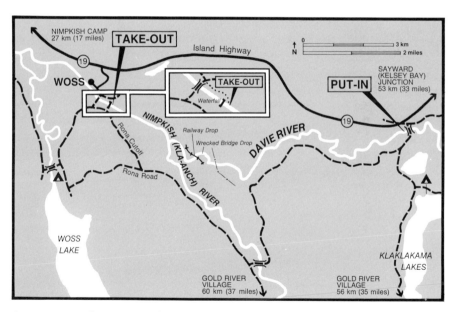

**Access to take-out and put-in:** Turn off Island Highway 19 into Woss. Head downhill for 1.1 kilometers (0.7 mile), cross the railway tracks, turn left, and go to a bridge over the Nimpkish (Kla-anch): the take-out.

For the put-in, return to Highway 19, turn right and go 10.5 kilometers (6.5 miles) to a gravel road with the signpost "Mount Cain, Vernon Camp and Schoen Lake Park". Then turn right and follow the sign toward Schoen Lake to a bridge over the Davie.

# NIMPKISH (KLA-ANCH) RIVER
## *Duncan Road Bridge to Woss*

**Who:** Intermediate and advanced kayakers, and guided novices; intermediate and expert open-canoeists; rafters

**Water to expect:** Class 2, 2+ and 3; it builds. An optional Class 4 or 5 waterfall or fish ladder. Medium volume, straightforward, and a steady gradient

**Length of run:** 8.2 kilometers (5.1 miles); 3 hours

**Shuttle one way:** 7.9 kilometers (4.9 miles); 10 minutes. Gravel logging road

**Why go:** A laid-back but lively intermediate run with surfing waves, boulders, and rock gardens. A waterfall and a fish ladder for those who want quick thrills are at the end of this pretty, fun stretch.

**Topographic Map:** 1:50,000 Woss Lake 92L/2.

**Facilities:** Picnic tables, pit toilets, and fire rings are provided free at the campground beside Woss Lake.

**Guidelines:** Dashing through froth beneath the put-in bridge would have made my day even if there were no other interest on this river. All water! Rocks funnel it into an hourglass, squeezing it down from 40- to 15-meter (130- to 50-foot) width; pushing it into a series of three bouncy fun waves. A placid Class 2 stretch follows, but when we were there the sun was shining and the joy of the first chute was still with us when we reached riffles; then surfing waves, boulders, and rock gardens.

The river broadens to 80 meters (260 feet) at the take-out. Gradient averages a gentle 4 meters/kilometer (20 feet/mile) overall, yet the run climaxes, for those who want it, with a sometimes-runnable 2- to 3-meter (6-to 10-foot) high waterfall or a zany fish ladder around it. A big eddy above them: approach with caution because conditions change daily. Expert judgment is required to determine when either is runnable, as well as skill to pull it off. And it helps if you're having a good day. When we first paddled the Nimpkish, two of our group ran the fish ladder; on that trip I was satisfied with our time on the river, skipped the last drop, and simply climbed up the right bank, which is easy to do. On the next trip I did run the falls and liked the experience. However, I am still plucking up courage to run that fish ladder. The Nimpkish is truly a river with something for everyone for run after run after run.

**Access to take-out and put-in:** To reach the take-out, turn off Island Highway 19 into Woss. Head downhill for 1.1 kilometers (0.7 mile), cross the

**Season:** Year-round; best from October through June. Rain-fed and snow-melt. I paddled it in late May; precise riverflow data unavailable; my guess is 75 m$^3$/s (2650 cfs)

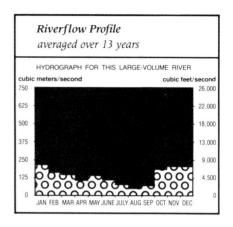

*Riverflow Profile*
*averaged over 13 years*

HYDROGRAPH FOR THIS LARGE-VOLUME RIVER

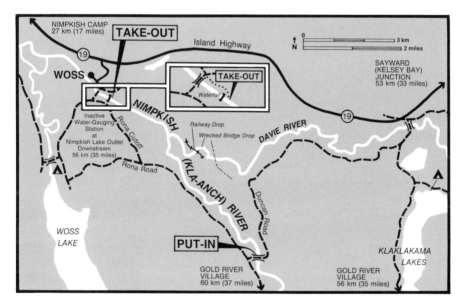

railway tracks, turn left, and go to a big bridge over the Nimpkish.

For the put-in, cross the bridge and turn left up the first gravel road you reach, Rona Cutoff. When Rona Road joins it, continue straight for 4.7 kilometers (2.9 miles) more; then turn left into Duncan Road and go a short distance to the put-in bridge.

Travel usually is permitted 24 hours a day on these private industrial roads. However, logging traffic could be on them too, so always drive with your headlights on. The best times to use them are weekends, holidays, and weekdays before 7 a.m. and after 5 p.m. To learn about possible fire-hazard closures, contact Canadian Forest Products, Woss, B.C. V0N 3P0, telephone (604)974-5551.

# NIMPKISH (KLA-ANCH) RIVER
## *Kaipit Creek to Nimpkish Camp*

**Who:** All kayakers; guided novice and intermediate open-canoeists; rafters

**Water to expect:** Class 2, a short Class 2+ rapid, and flat water

**Length of run:** 16.9 kilometers (10.5 miles) of river and 0.5 kilometer (⅓ mile) of lake; 3 hours

**Shuttle one way:** 17.8 kilometers (11.0 miles); 20 minutes. Gravel logging road for 10.0 kilometers (6.2 miles) of it

**Season:** Year-round; best after rain. We paddled it in late May; precise riverflow

**Why go:** Iron Mine Rapid is the highlight of this run: an excellent series of six or seven good-sized standing waves — and nothing else in the way. Just waves. Enjoy! A fun rapid for both seasoned paddlers and novices. A safe place for kayakers to start learning to surf on the river because the water is unimpeded and "clean": sweepers are unlikely (but check for them), and there are no rocks to bash if you swim or roll. Immediately below Iron Mine, a pool. Beyond that is a scenic tour: gorgeous limestone caverns curving out over the slow dark water; deep black pools partly revealing huge submerged "house rocks"; ledges tapering to where you cannot see. Then the river opens out to broad gravel bars and sandy beaches: good places to stop for lunch in the sun. We saw a harbor seal when paddling the final stretch along the southern shore of Nimpkish Lake.

This is a superb section of river for unguided novices who want to make a first run "on their own".

**Topographic Maps:** 1:50,000 Woss Lake 92L/2 and Nimpkish 92L/7.

**Facilities:** Picnic tables, pit toilets, and fire rings provided free at campgrounds beside nearby Woss Lake and Anutz Lake, and at Cheslakees Campground where the highway turns left toward Port McNeill.

**Guidelines:** A short run down Kaipit Creek to the river, then a third of the way on it around a bend to the left you will see Iron Mine Rapid. Waves were 1 meter (3 feet) high when we paddled here. You may want to climb out on the left to look at this series of "haystacks", or walk around it. After Iron Mine Rapid, it's easy to scout from the water all the way to the lake.

Riverflow usually ranges between 100 and 175 m³/s (3530 to 6180 cfs) from October through June, making the Nimpkish (Kla-anch) the largest-volume river on Vancouver Island. An alarming maximum recorded flow of 1270 m³/s (44,900 cfs) occurred on December 31, 1926. However, most of the way and most of the time, this is a languid stream. The gradient averages

data unavailable; my guess is 90 m$^3$/s (3180 cfs)

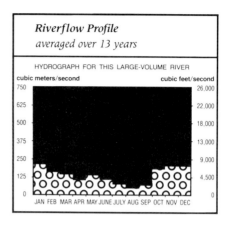

**Riverflow Profile**
*averaged over 13 years*

HYDROGRAPH FOR THIS LARGE-VOLUME RIVER

| cubic meters/second | | cubic feet/second |
|---|---|---|
| 750 | | 26,000 |
| 625 | | 22,000 |
| 500 | | 18,000 |
| 375 | | 13,000 |
| 250 | | 9,000 |
| 125 | | 4,500 |
| 0 | | 0 |

JAN FEB MAR APR MAY JUNE JULY AUG SEP OCT NOV DEC

only 3 meters/kilometer (15 feet/mile); there are few obstructions; and width ranges up to 100 meters (330 feet). Broad and clean — it's a lazy giant.

*At Cheslakees Campground*

*Drifting over submerged "house rocks"*

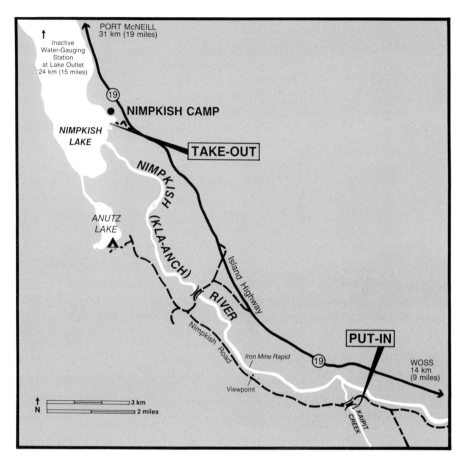

**Access to take-out and put-in:** Turn off Island Highway 19 into Nimpkish Camp and head downhill to Nimpkish Lake. Bear left past a gas station, turn right, cross two pairs of railway tracks, pass the fire hall, and turn left downhill. Make a hairpin turn to the right. Then turn left and you are at the take-out.

To reach the put-in, return to Highway 19, turn right, and go 6.3 kilometers (3.9 miles) to a gravel logging road on the left. Go off on it, turn right, and cross a bridge over the highway. Continue through the logging camp shop area, cross a bridge over the Nimpkish, and turn left. From the bridge, it is 4.0 kilometers (2.5 miles) to Iron Mine viewpoint; the same distance again to the put-in at Kaipit Creek.

---

Travel usually is permitted 24 hours a day on these private industrial roads. However, logging traffic might be on them too, so always drive with your headlights on. The best times to use them are on weekends, holidays, and weekdays before 7 a.m. and after 5 p.m. To learn about possible fire-hazard closures, contact Canadian Forest Products, Woss, B.C. V0N 3P0, telephone (604)974-5551.

# SAN JOSEF BAY
## Ocean Surf

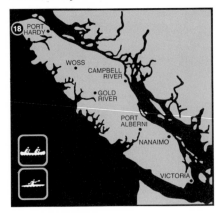

**Who:** All kayakers on 1-meter (3-foot) high waves; intermediate and advanced kayakers with Eskimo roll on larger ones. Expert open-canoeists on waves up to 1 meter (3 feet) high. No rafters

**Water to expect:** Varies from flat up to 2 or 3 meters (6 to 10 feet) high. A very gently shelving sandy beach

**Length of run:** Depending on wave height, the surf breaks from at least 100 meters (300 feet) offshore to the beach

**Shuttle one way:** None required

**Why go:** Quality of surf — when it's happening — is excellent. Great swells roll in from the open Pacific to the wide crescent of sand at San Josef Bay. No islands offshore to break it up. When small, the waves are smooth because the beach is so gently shelving; when large, they give you a long ride on a foamy breaker. Small waves when we were there; however each one offered a superbly "clean break" starting at one end of the wave and running across it. Larger waves are more erratic. No rocks on the beach; the few logs are not a problem; only a short walk across the sand: an ideal situation for learning to surf.

Wilderness beach camping at San Josef Bay is unsurpassed by any I have experienced in British Columbia. The only people other than boaters you will meet here have hiked in: no road access to this unspoiled bay. While there, we were lucky to enjoy 30°C (86°F) sunshine. While paddling out up the San Josef River we saw a bear with two cubs.

**Topographic Map and Tide Tables:** 1:50,000 San Josef 102I/9, and *Canadian Tide & Current Tables, Volume 6, Barkley Sound and Discovery Passage to Dixon Entrance*; refer to Tofino daily tables.

**Facilities:** Picnic tables, pit toilets, and fire rings provided free at campgrounds beside the San Josef River. Undeveloped camping space all over the sand at the nearly deserted beach at San Josef Bay which is 1½ kilometers (1 mile) long; however, it is difficult to find a clearing under the shelter of trees. Take a good tent.

**Guidelines:** We paddled against the tide going down the Class 1 San Josef River to reach the beach and paddling up it again; no problem — but for the easiest possible circumstances, plan to head downriver when the ocean tide is flowing out and be ready to surf on the incoming tide. Then paddle upriver when the tide is on the way in. After surfing, rinse your gear in the freshwater river.

**Season:** Year-round; best in August and September when the water is warmer. Biggest waves after it is stormy out at sea. I kayak-surfed it in late May on an incoming tide with waves up to ½ meter (1½ feet) high

*San Josef Bay*

Before heading out to the San Josef, load up with provisions at Port Hardy: some groceries are available in nearby Holberg. However, don't count on anything specific: accept what comes. We enjoyed a sumptuous breakfast there served by a burly logger in a cafe with white ruffled curtains.

*Past this crossroad, the right fork*

Barnacled rocks, wide crescent of sand behind

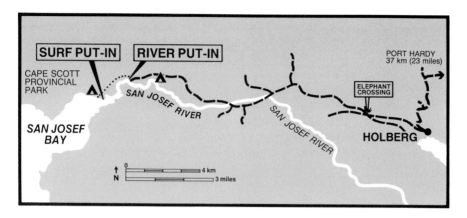

**Access to river put-in and to surf put-in:** There is no road access to San Josef Bay which is in Cape Scott Provincial Park. From Port Hardy to the end of the road at San Josef River is a 1½-hour drive. From there, it's a 15-minute paddle down the languorous river to the surf.

To reach the river, drive from Port Hardy on good gravel forest-access roads past Nahwitti Lake, then on logging roads to Holberg. If you stop at the logging company's office in Holberg, someone will radio a message to trucks to watch for you on the roads from there. On leaving Holberg, go west to a logging crossroad with the signpost "Elephant Crossing". Immediately past this sign, follow the right fork. Various roads branch off, but keep to the main one, crossing the river twice on the way, and drive to the end of the road. Then paddle a short distance downriver to the ocean and put in on the surf.

---

Travel on private industrial roads west of Nahwitti Lake is subject to restriction at any time, but usually is permitted 24 hours a day. However, there could be logging traffic too, so always drive with your headlights on. Observe these signposts at road entries:

Red: Active logging area that is open to the public only on weekends, holidays, and weekdays before 7 a.m. and after 5 p.m.

Yellow: Open to the public but also used by heavy vehicles. Drive with extreme caution and always yield to logging traffic.

Green: Open to the public except during fire-hazard closures.

To learn about possible closures and to inform drivers of radio-controlled vehicles that you will be using the access roads, contact Western Forest Products, Holberg, B. C. V0N 1Z0, telephone (604)288-3362.

# MARBLE RIVER
## *Lake Outlet Falls to Coal Harbour*

**Who:** Intermediate and advanced kayakers, and guided novices; no open-canoeists; no rafters

**Water to expect:** Class 2, some Class 3, a Class 5 drop (portageable) and two mandatory portages. River probably dangerous, or even unrunnable, at high winter levels. Falls, pools, falls; then flatwater ocean paddling

**Length of run:** 7.6 kilometers (4.7 miles) of river and 9.0 kilometers (5.6 miles) of ocean; 4 hours on the river and 1½ hours on the sea

**Why go:** Promises of aqua water so clear you're frightened you'll fall through it lured me to this beautiful canyon river with alternating falls, pools, and more falls. When it has moderate flow and is not too pushy, as we found it, Marble River is a perfect place to practice spotting the glassy pools that precede waterfalls.

The river is mostly just a beautiful float; there is one Class 3 rapid; the rest is Class 2. In the lower canyon we saw deep pools with huge boulders in them. Alongside are natural limestone arches, columns, water-carved caverns. Tidal marshland is the final part of the river run; then open-ocean paddling; and an interesting village to poke around in at the end of your trip. Coal Harbour was the last active whaling station on the West Coast of Canada, and the take-out is the ramp where whales were hauled out until the station was closed in 1970.

**Topographic Maps:** 1:50,000 Port McNeill 92L/11 and Quatsino 92L/12.

**Facilities:** Free campsites with picnic tables, pit toilets, and fire rings at the put-in. Tasty rainbow trout in the stream.

**Guidelines:** Pick a sunny day for this scenic paddle when the water is clear, clean, and dropping. River width ranges radically from 4 to 40 meters (13 to 130 feet). The gradient averages 7 meters/kilometer (35 feet/mile). Some water is diverted from the lower Marble to a nearby mine, but not in a great enough quantity to be noticed by boaters. Assess riverflow here as you would any other naturally flowing river that responds to rain and is moderated by a lake above it. If you suspect flow could be too high, check it out by walking along the fisherman's trail on the left bank from the campground downstream: 2½ kilometers (1½ miles) to the first constricted drops in the upper canyon. If no recent heavy rains, climb into your boats, and scout from the river.

The sequence of drops: A couple of rapids to run just past the put-in below Lake Outlet Falls, then a pattern of falls and pools down to the sea. Our first

**Shuttle one way:** 29.2 kilometers (18.1 miles); 1 hour. Pavement for 10.8 kilometers (6.7 miles); gravel logging roads for 18.4 kilometers (11.4 miles)

**Season:** Year-round, but avoid extremely high water. Best when dropping after spring runoff: May and June. Rain-fed and snow-melt; stabilized by lakes above the run. We paddled it in late May; precise riverflow data unavailable; my guess is 34 m³/s (1200 cfs)

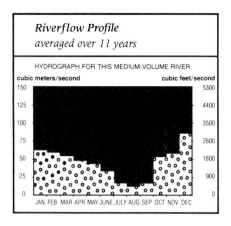

*Riverflow Profile*
*averaged over 11 years*

HYDROGRAPH FOR THIS MEDIUM-VOLUME RIVER

| cubic meters/second | cubic feet/second |
| --- | --- |
| 150 | 5300 |
| 125 | 4400 |
| 100 | 3500 |
| 75 | 2600 |
| 50 | 1800 |
| 25 | 900 |
| 0 | 0 |

JAN FEB MAR APR MAY JUNE JULY AUG SEP OCT NOV DEC

portage was in the upper canyon: a narrow, slotted Class 5 drop. Shortly downstream from that drop, when the river broadens, the shore flattens and the scene becomes innocent looking — watch out! You are approaching Bear Falls, the most impressive waterfall on the run and one of the listed mandatory portages. It may be runnable with higher flow, but in any event it must be spotted: be alert for a too-smooth glassy look. That is the only warning you have of this cascade which drops abruptly 3 to 4 meters (10 to 13 feet). But it's easy to carry around.

The next noticeable spot is a huge undercut cavern where the river sweeps left. It was an unthreatening, invitingly cool place at the level we saw it, but would be potentially dangerous with high flow. Shortly past the cavern we

*Below Bear Falls*

carried our boats around a log that blocked the narrow lower canyon. That log may be gone now, or there may be more. Your only protection against this sort of hazard is to paddle under control throughout the run, always with two eddies ahead that you are confident you can catch.

The last mandatory portage is in the steeply walled canyon at Twin Falls. The upper falls drops 1¼ meters (4 feet); the lower falls, twice that much. The two are separated by 30 meters (100 feet) of flat water. We carried our kayaks around both of them. A short rapid follows, and then you are into the barnacled tidal zone. Before starting across the inlet, stretch your legs. When you reach Coal Harbour, rinse your boat and gear with fresh water.

*Portaging*

**Access to take-out and put-in:** From Port Hardy, drive south to Coal Harbour — when you pass the signpost ''A Whale of a Town'' you're there. Head to the waterfront. The old whaling-station ramp at the right of the government dock is the easiest place to take out.

For the put-in, return toward Port Hardy for 6.6 kilometers (4.1 miles). Turn right onto a paved road with a signpost to Utah Mines, then immediately left and right into a gravel industrial road. Keep going straight and in 9.7 kilometers (6.0 miles) you will see the head of Rupert Inlet. Continue south, crossing Washlawlis Creek, passing a road to Port McNeill, and crossing Waukwaas Creek (Rupert River). When you reach Port Alice Highway, turn right and go to a bridge over the Marble River. Cross the bridge and immediately turn right into the campground; put in just below Lake Outlet Falls.

---

Travel on private industrial roads in this area usually is permitted 24 hours a day; however, there could be logging traffic too. Always drive with your headlights on. Observe these signposts at road entries:

Red: Active logging area that is open to the public only on weekends, holidays, and weekdays before 7 a.m. and after 5 p.m.

Yellow: Open to the public but also used by heavy vehicles. Drive with extreme

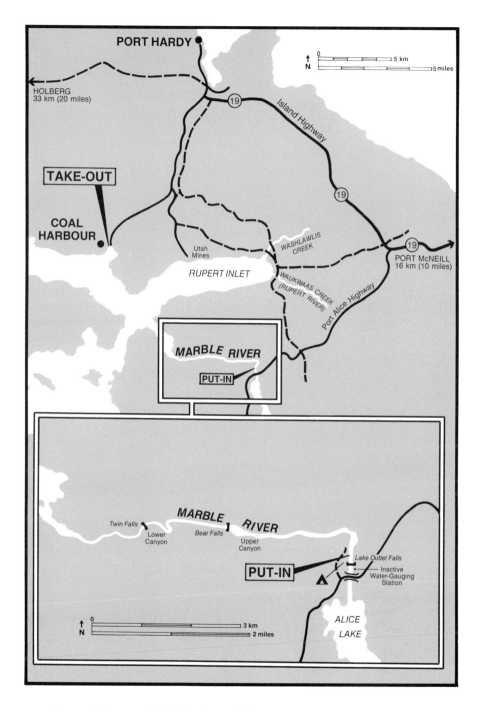

caution and always yield to logging traffic.

Green: Public welcome except during fire-hazard closures.

To learn if there are closures, contact MacMillan Bloedel, Port McNeill, B.C. V0N 2R0, telephone (604)956-4416.

# GOLD RIVER
## The Upper Canyon

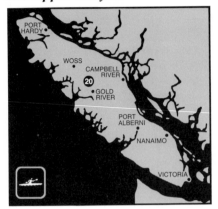

**Who:** Advanced kayakers and guided intermediates; no open-canoeists; no rafters

**Water to expect:** Class 3+ and 4+. At high levels, Class 5. Technical pool-and-drop river; incredible play spots

**Length of run:** 6.1 kilometers (3.8 miles); 4 hours

**Shuttle one way:** 6.0 kilometers (3.7 miles); 10 minutes. Gravel road

**Season:** Year-round following rain. Best when dropping after runoff: May and June. Rain-fed and snow-melt. We

**Why go:** A gorgeous canyon: remote yet easy to reach. Eagles, salmon, and kayaks are all that can negotiate it. Excellent water: continuous rapids, then pools and drops with superb holes to play in; and the drops become more difficult, more beautiful, the deeper you penetrate this narrowing canyon.

The best play spots with the least amount of driving — on Vancouver Island.

**Topographic Map:** 1:50,000 Gold River 92E/16.

**Facilities:** Space to pitch your tent, pit toilets, and room to park are provided free at Gold River Campsite. You will also find a beautiful sandy beach, shade trees, picnic tables, pit toilets and fireplaces at the picnic site in Big Bend Park. Both are south of town toward Muchalat Inlet.

**Guidelines:** Best in early afternoon when sun shines into the deep canyon. Width is 24 meters (80 feet) at the Muchalat River put-in; once on the Gold, sometimes it is as narrow as 3 meters (10 feet). No choices at some chutes. Gradient averages only 7 meters/kilometer (35 feet/mile), but do not be fooled; radical narrowing creates exciting water. At high levels, play spots galore; at lower levels, some drops become extremely difficult. Although the entire canyon was runnable, I chose to portage several drops. Scout carefully: in tight space like this a fallen log could become a "terminal tree". Check it.

paddled it in late May with riverflow of 55 m³/s (1940 cfs)

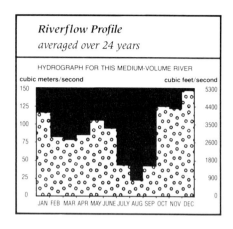

**Riverflow Profile**
*averaged over 24 years*

HYDROGRAPH FOR THIS MEDIUM-VOLUME RIVER

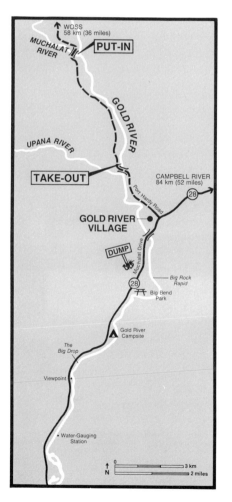

**Access to take-out and put-in:** When in the town of Gold River, turn off Highway 28 (Muchalat Drive) onto Port Hardy Road. Go north to the first bridge over Gold River. Cross it and park. Just past the bridge and a signpost, walk down the short, steep, rocky edge of the road, then along a trail through the trees to the water. A good eddy above the bridge is the take-out.

To put in, continue upstream to another bridge, this one over Muchalat River. Cross it. Turn right, then right again: a dirt track goes all the way to the water.

*In the canyon*

# GOLD RIVER
## Middle Section

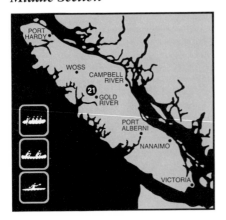

**Who:** All kayakers; intermediate and expert open-canoeists; rafters

**Water to expect:** Class 2+ and a Class 3+ boulder drop (portageable). Short rapids with a steady gradient; drops and pools

**Length of run:** 9.7 kilometers (6.0 miles); 4 hours

**Shuttle one way:** 7.4 kilometers (4.6 miles); 15 minutes. Gravel road for one-third of it; the rest is pavement

**Season:** Year-round; best in May and June. Rain-fed and snow-melt. I

**Why go:** Emerald pools alternate with lively, yet straightforward rapids, rock gardens, and drops to a demanding boulder drop at Big Rock Rapid. Good play waves, sandy beaches, and eagles along this relatively "clean" (usually sweeper-free) stretch with an easy shuttle. The river flows right through town. However, in a boat you feel miles from anywhere.

**Topographic Maps:** 1:50,000 Gold River 92E/16 and Muchalat Inlet 92E/9.

**Facilities:** A beautiful sandy beach, shade trees, picnic tables, pit toilets, and fireplaces three-fourths of the way along the run in Big Bend Park. Space to pitch your tent, pit toilets and room to park are provided free at the take-out at Gold River Campsite. The nearby garbage dump is a popular spot for viewing bears, but you may not need to go there: while eating breakfast, we watched a black bear ambling past on the mountainside behind the campground. If you are heading east toward Campbell River, camping is available (for a fee during peak season) at Buttle Lake Provincial Park, which is 36 kilometers (22 miles) away; or continue 8 kilometers (5 miles) more and drop in for a meal, a sauna, or just to look around at Strathcona Park Lodge.

**Guidelines:** Soon after putting in, you'll find that the river bends left into an evenly descending Class 2+ rapid which ends in a deep pool, then turns sharply left between high canyon walls. Drops and pools continue throughout the run. Past the bridge in town look for Big Rock Rapid. If your group includes novices, or if the water is high, it is a good idea to climb out and scout. You will recognize this spot when you see huge boulders scattered across the river, and it is easy to portage around it on the right bank. Beyond Big Rock Rapid, are one or two more drops, Big Bend Park, and the take-out.

River width is 30 to 45 meters (100 to 150 feet); gradient averages 10 meters/kilometer (55 feet/mile). A beautiful and exciting run for beginner and novice paddlers during low water; basic kayaking courses are taught on it by Strathcona Park Lodge from midsummer to late summer. During spring

paddled it in mid-August, mid-July, and late May with riverflows of 10, 14, and 53 m³/s (350, 490, and 1870 cfs)

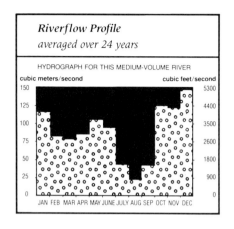

**Riverflow Profile**
*averaged over 24 years*

HYDROGRAPH FOR THIS MEDIUM-VOLUME RIVER

cubic meters/second · cubic feet/second

runoff, and when winter rains raise the river, it is fun for advanced paddlers. At very high levels, everything goes up a grade: the overall river rating becomes Class 3+ and Big Rock Rapid is Class 4+. Since 1979, Gold River has been the site of whitewater races at an October invitational sponsored by Strathcona Park Lodge.

*Emerald pools*

*Canyon wall*

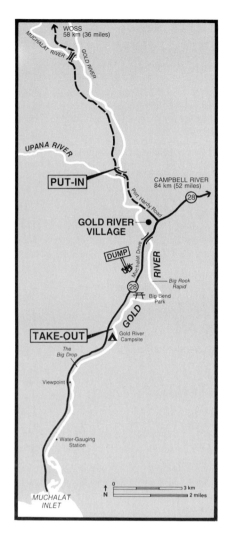

**Access to take-out and put-in:** From the town of Gold River, head south on Muchalat Drive (Highway 28) to Gold River Campsite; when we were there no sign marked it. Measure the distance: drive 3.7 kilometers (2.3 miles) beyond the bridge in town to the wide gravel parking area; turn in at the top end of it, go to the river, and flag the take-out.

To put in, return through town along Muchalat Drive to the junction. One signpost points straight toward Campbell River; another points left toward Port Hardy. Turn left. The road soon becomes gravel; continue on it to the first bridge. Cross it and park. Just past the bridge and a signpost, walk down the short, steep, rocky edge of the road; then along a trail through the trees to the put-in.

*After paddling, music and boat-repairing time at Strathcona Park Lodge*

# GOLD RIVER
## *The Lower Canyon*

**Who:** Intermediate and advanced kayakers; no open-canoeists; intermediate and advanced rafters. At low levels, also guided novice kayakers; expert open-canoeists; and novice rafters

**Water to expect:** Class 2 and 3, and a Class 4 boulder drop; medium volume and technical. At peak levels, Class 3+ and a Class 4+ big-water drop

**Length of run:** 5.8 kilometers (3.6 miles); 1 to 2 hours, depending on play time

**Shuttle one way:** 5.5 kilometers

**Why go:** For The Big Drop — the biggest-water boating experience on Vancouver Island. In addition, there are a few surfing waves, one or two good holes to play in — and some to avoid! The entire section is scenic with waterfalls spilling in, a natural gate in the rock, eagles. Wild columbine and strawberries.

A compact run, with super-easy access.

**Topographic Map:** 1:50,000 Muchalat Inlet 92E/9.

**Facilities:** Space to pitch your tent, pit toilets, and room to park provided free at Gold River Campsite put-in. A beautiful sandy beach, shade trees, picnic tables, pit toilets and fireplaces in Big Bend Park picnic area. Slightly closer to town is the Gold River garbage dump, a popular spot for viewing bears.

**Guidelines:** The full run is short, so play at all holes and surfing waves along the way. Beyond the natural gate of rock, when you see a prominent waterfall spouting from the right cliff and a couple of large gravel bars ahead on "river left", expect The Big Drop around the next corner. It goes for 350 meters (1150 feet). Serious . . . exciting! Eddy out on the right to scout. When we paddled through the lower canyon, a gigantic hole was across the right half of the river at the bottom of the most intense stretch of white water. We punched through a curling green roller at the entry to the drop and, keeping left, made a straight shot through solid white. Big waves, up to 1½ meters (5 feet) high when we paddled there.

Past the huge hole, an obvious green tongue cuts through the second set of waves. Then the river relents, flows quietly between steep canyon walls, and the banks become lower. Run through a few waves at corners and you are at the take-out. If you reach orange cones hanging over the river (aircraft warning markers on the water-gauging station cableway) you have gone too far. It is a short walk back to the parking area.

The Gold was broad and "clean" when we ran it. River width averages

(3.4 miles); 5 minutes. Paved highway

**Season:** Year-round. Biggest water during spring runoff, May and June, and at October peak. I paddled it in mid-June with riverflow of 140 m³/s (4950 cfs)

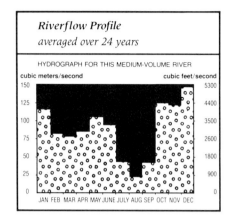

*Riverflow Profile*
*averaged over 24 years*

HYDROGRAPH FOR THIS MEDIUM-VOLUME RIVER

| cubic meters/second | | cubic feet/second |
| --- | --- | --- |

JAN FEB MAR APR MAY JUNE JULY AUG SEP OCT NOV DEC

45 meters (150 feet); but it becomes as narrow as 8 meters (26 feet) at the natural gate. Gradient averages 7 meters/kilometer (35 feet/mile); however this is not indicative of the degree of difficulty throughout the run, because most of the vertical descent comes at The Big Drop where there is also narrowing: it's interesting to see it on the topographic map. At lower water, The Big Drop is a technical boulder-ledge with huge pools spaced between drops. The lower canyon is a good morning run — that's when the sun hits it.

*Preparing to play*

*The Big Drop*

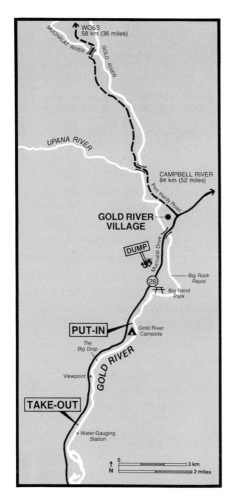

**Access to take-out and put-in:**
From the town of Gold River, head south on Muchalat Drive (Highway 28). Go 9.2 kilometers (5.7 miles) past the bridge in town to the take-out. You are nearing it when you crest a hill and see smoke billowing over the pulp mill. At the bottom of the hill, turn left into a large parking area. The take-out is not easy to see from the river, so you may want to place a marker.

To reach the put-in, return toward the town of Gold River. When 2.7 kilometers (1.7 miles) upstream from the take-out, pull off to the right into a lay-by and view The Big Drop; then continue 2.7 kilometers (1.7 miles) more to Gold River Campsite and put in.

*Play time*

# WHITEWATER INFORMATION SOURCES

## 1. TOURIST INFORMATION FOR BRITISH COLUMBIA

### Road Maps, Campgrounds and Other Accommodations, and Facilities

Tourism British Columbia
1117 Wharf Street
Victoria, B.C. V8V 2Z2
(604)387-1642
Vancouver: (604)668-2300
*Provincial road map and accommodation guide*

Province of British Columbia
Parks and Outdoor Recreation Division
Ministry of Lands, Parks and Housing
1019 Wharf Street
Victoria, B.C. V8W 2Y9
(604)387-5044
*A map locating and describing provincial parks and campgrounds and listing facilities including publications describing parks noted for canoeing*

Parks Canada
Information Directorate
Suite 401
1001 West Pender Street
Vancouver, B.C. V6E 2M7
(604)666-6058
*A road and facilities map of Pacific Rim National Park and Kootenay National Park as well as information on all federal parks and a camping guide*

Outdoor Recreation Council of British Columbia
1200 Hornby Street
Vancouver, B.C. V6Z 2E2
(604)687-3333
*A series of 1:100,000 topographic maps locating public and commercial campgrounds, services, and a variety of outdoor recreational facilities ($3.95 each)*

### Ferries

British Columbia Ferry Corporation
1045 Howe Street
Vancouver, B.C. V6Z 2A9
(604)669-1211
Victoria:(604)386-3431
Seattle: (206)682-6865
Toll-free Campbell River and northward for Prince Rupert
reservations: Zenith 2020
*Information on ferries between:*
*Vancouver (Tsawwassen)—Gulf Islands—Swartz Bay (Victoria)*
*West Vancouver (Horseshoe Bay)—Departure Bay (Nanaimo)*
*Vancouver (Tsawwassen)—Port Hardy—Prince Rupert (summer only)*
*Port Hardy—Prince Rupert (year-round)*

British Columbia Steamship Company
390 Belleville Street
Victoria, B.C. V8V 1W9
(604)386-1124 or 388-7397
*Ferries (May through October) between Victoria and Seattle*

Black Ball Transport
430 Belleville Street
Victoria, B.C. V8V 1W9
(604)386-2202
*Ferries between Victoria and Port Angeles, Washington*

Washington State Ferries
Blaney Terminals Ltd., Agents
2499 Ocean Avenue
Sidney, B.C. V8L 1T3
(604)381-1551 or 656-1531
*Ferries between Sidney (Victoria), the San Juan Islands, and Anacortes, Washington*

Marine Superintendent
Ministry of Transportation and Highways
940 Blanshard Street
Victoria, B.C. V8W 3E6
(604)387-3996
Vancouver: (604)525-0961, radio room
*Free ferries between:*
*Fort Langley–Albion (Fraser Valley)*
*Boston Bar–North Bend (Fraser Canyon)*
*Shelter Bay–Galena (West Kootenays)*
*Needles–Fauquier (West Kootenays)*
*Balfour–Kootenay Bay (West Kootenays)*

## 2. CLUBS AND COURSES

Taking a course is an excellent way to start paddling. Then, join in club activities to find people to paddle with and to develop paddling skills. Since whitewater boating is a fast-growing sport, new clubs are frequently formed. In addition, the person to contact regarding club activities may change from year to year. Courses are conducted by member associations of Canoe Sport British Columbia, and by private instructors, many of whom are certified by the appropriate association listed below. For current information about clubs and courses in your area contact:

Canoe Sport British Columbia
1200 Hornby Street
Vancouver, B.C. V6Z 2E2
(604)687-3333

Member Associations:
  Whitewater Canoeing Association
  of British Columbia (Kayaking)
  Recreational Canoeing Association
  of British Columbia (Open-Canoeing)
  Olympic Canoeing and Kayaking,
  Pacific Division (Olympic Racing, flatwater)

At present there is no formal association of recreational rafting clubs in British Columbia. However, some professional rafters welcome kayakers on their trips. For information regarding professional rafting trips contact:

River Outfitters Association of British Columbia
1200 Hornby Street
Vancouver, B.C. V6Z 2E2
(604)687-3333

---

**Learn to Kayak**

Action River Expeditions Ltd.
5389 Southeast Marine Drive
Burnaby, B.C. V5J 3G7
(604)437-6679

Nimbus Paddles Ltd.
2330 Tyner Street, Unit 6
Port Coquitlam, B.C. V3C 2Z1
(604)941-8138

Ocean River Sports
560 Johnson Street
166 North Market Square
Victoria, B.C. V8W 3C6
(604)381-4233

Outward Bound
Suite 101
1600 West 6th Avenue
Vancouver, B.C. V6J 1R3
(604)733-9104

Similkameen Wilderness Centre
P.O. Box 97
Cultus Lake, B.C. V0X 1H0
(604)858-6775

Snowbird Mountaineering
P.O. Box 910
Smithers, B.C. V0J 2N0
(604)847-4876

Strathcona Park Lodge and
    Outdoor Education Centre
P.O. Box 2160
Campbell River, B.C. V9W 5C9
Dial 0 and ask for Campbell River
    radiotelephone; then ask for
    Strathcona Lodge N693546

University of Victoria
Recreation Department
P.O. Box 1700
Victoria, B.C. V8W 2Y2
(604)721-8406

Vancouver Parks and Recreation
Lord Byng Pool
3990 West 14th Avenue
Vancouver, B.C. V6R 4H2
(604)228-9735

West Coast Paddling School
746 Sea Drive, R.R. 1
Brentwood Bay, B.C. V0S 1A0
(604)652-0409

West Vancouver Aquatic Centre
776 Twenty-Second Street
West Vancouver, B.C. V7V 4B9
(604)926-8585

Whistler Whitewater
P.O. Box 345
Whistler, B.C. V0N 1B0
(604)932-3262

YMCA-YWCA
880 Courtney Street
Victoria, B.C. V8W 1C4
(604)386-7511

---

## Learn to Canoe

Capilano College
Outdoor Recreation Department
2055 Purcell Way
North Vancouver, B.C. V7J 3H5
(604)986-1911

Outward Bound
Suite 101
1600 West 6th Avenue
Vancouver, B.C. V6J 1R3
(604)733-9104

Strathcona Park Lodge and
    Outdoor Education Centre
P.O. Box 2160
Campbell River, B.C. V9W 5C9
Dial 0 and ask for Campbell River
    radiotelephone; then ask for
    Strathcona Lodge N693546

University of Victoria
Recreation Department
P.O. Box 1700
Victoria, B.C. V8W 2Y2
(604)721-8406

West Coast Paddling School
746 Sea Drive, R.R. 1
Brentwood Bay, B.C. V0S 1A0
(604)652-0409

YMCA-YWCA
880 Courtney Street
Victoria, B.C. V8W 1C4
(604)386-7511

---

## Learn to Raft

Action River Expeditions Ltd.
5389 Southeast Marine Drive
Burnaby, B.C. V5J 3G7
(604)437-6679

# 3. BOOKS, MAGAZINES, PAMPHLETS

Kayakers, canoeists, and rafters will find many facts in the following list of books and periodicals that is especially selected to complement the where-to-go data in this guidebook. There is information about techniques, tactics, and equipment, about reading water, and about ocean currents and riptides.

## BOOKS

*Canoeing and Kayaking* published by the American Red Cross Canoeing Advisory Committee in cooperation with the Training Committee of the American Canoe Association. 1981. The American National Red Cross, National Headquarters, Washington, D.C. 20006. 242 pages. Equipment, strokes, training drills (including English gate), tactics, rescue, and river reading for open-canoeists and kayakers. An excellent, comprehensive how-to manual for all whitewater boaters. It is well illustrated with drawings.

*The Kayaking Book* by Jay Evans. 1983. The Stephen Greene Press, Brattleboro, Vermont. 288 pages. A complete manual for closed-boaters: starts with historical facts about kayaks and kayaking. Covers essentials on boats, paddles, gear, and techniques for whitewater river running in a kayak (K-1 or K-2), C-1 and C-2; also ocean surfing. Excellent photographs.

*Oceanography of the B.C. Coast* by Richard Thomson. 1981. Department of Fisheries and Oceans, Ottawa. 291 pages. A scientific — yet easy-to-read — reference book containing information about currents and riptides. Well illustrated with photographs and drawings.

*Path of the Paddle* by Bill Mason. 1980. Van Nostrand Reinhold Ltd., Toronto and New York. 200 pages. For beginner to expert open-canoeists: a practical book, but also beautiful. It contains clearly written descriptions of basic strokes, and a photo series showing how to do each stroke; intriguing drawing and photo combinations showing how to read water; and alluring color photographs of rivers for all to enjoy. An exceptional picture book.

*River Rescue* by Ohio Department of Natural Resources, Division of Watercraft. 1980. The Vocational Instructional Materials Laboratory, The Ohio State University, Columbus, Ohio. 108 pages. Information on river reading and tactics for everyday river running are included in this training manual along with techniques for self-rescue, for rescuing other boaters, and for rescuing other boats from a dam, from a midstream obstruction such as a bridge pier, and from a strainer. Clear drawings show safe ways to effect rescues.

*River Running* by Verne Huser. 1975. Henry Regnery Company, Chicago. 294 pages. For rafters: a great deal of information on inflatable boats and equipment; some on technique. Illustrated.

*White Water Handbook* by John T. Urban, revised by T. Walley Williams III. 1981. Appalachian Mountain Club, 5 Joy Street, Boston. 198 pages. Fundamental strokes for open-canoeists, kayakers, C-1 and C-2 paddlers; river running, and rescue. Photographs and illustrations.

*The White-Water River Book* by Ron Watters. 1982. Pacific Search Press, Seattle, and Douglas & McIntyre Ltd., Vancouver. 204 pages. Includes information on technique, strategies, and equipment for kayakers and rafters; also excellent photographs, drawings, and descriptions on reading water and on river safety for all river-runners. Rich graphics.

*Whitewater Rafting* by William McGinnis. 1975. Quadrangle/The New York Times Book Co., New York, and Fitzhenry and Whiteside Ltd., Toronto. 361 pages. A well-illustrated comprehensive how-to guide for rafters.

*Wildwater* by Lito Tejada-Flores. 1978. Sierra Club Books, San Francisco. 329 pages. Techniques and equipment for kayakers and rafters. Drawings and a few photographs.

## MAGAZINES

*American Whitewater Journal*
American Whitewater Affiliation
146 North Brockway
Palatine, Illinois 60067
Bimonthly: for kayakers, canoeists, and rafters

*Canoe Magazine*
Highland Mill
Camden, Maine 04843
(207)236-9621
Bimonthly: for kayakers, canoeists, and rafters

*Canoeing*
Ocean Publications Ltd.
34 Buckingham Palace Road
London SW1W ORE
England
01-828 4551 extension 32
Monthly: for kayakers and canoeists

*Canoeist* (incorporating *White Water Magazine*)
13 Wellington Crescent
Baughurst
Basingstoke, Hants RG26 5PF
England
Monthly: for kayakers and canoeists

*Currents*
National Organization for River Sports (NORS)
P.O. Box 6847, 314 North 20th Street
Colorado Springs, Colorado 80934
(303)473-2466
Six times each year, March through winter: for kayakers, canoeists, and rafters

*River Runner*
P.O. Box 2047
Vista, California 92083
(619) 744-7170
Six times yearly: for kayakers, canoeists, and rafters

## PAMPHLETS

*Canoeing: A Guide to Safety in British Columbia* produced by the Outdoor Recreation Council of British Columbia, 1200 Hornby Street, Vancouver, B.C., V6Z 2E2. Eight pages. This pamphlet contains useful information about boats, hypothermia, and river ethics. To obtain a single free copy send a self-addressed envelope. Cost for quantities is $3 per 100.

*Kayaking: A Guide to Safety in British Columbia* produced by the Outdoor Recreation Council of British Columbia, 1200 Hornby Street, Vancouver, B.C., V6Z 2E2. Eight pages. This pamphlet contains useful information about boats, hypothermia, and river courtesy. To obtain a single free copy send a self-addressed envelope. Cost for quantities is $3 per 100.

*Safety Code* pamphlet by the American Whitewater Affiliation (AWA). Revised 1980. American Whitewater Affiliation, P.O. Box 1261, Jefferson City, Missouri 65102. Eight pages. Essential information: this guide to safe river boating in canoe, kayak, or raft is available in quantities of 50 at a low cost to cover printing and mailing. Send a self-addressed envelope for a single copy.

# 4. TOPOGRAPHIC MAPS, AIR PHOTOS, TIDE TABLES

## Topographic Maps

Both the federal and the provincial governments provide topographic maps in Canada.

The National Topographic System (NTS) is employed to organize all of these topographic maps ranging from the large-scale 1:50,000 series to the small-scale 1:500,000 series. Numbering of maps is the same for both the federal and the provincial editions; however, scale differs as does some of the information on the maps.

Provincial editions are usually more useful to boaters because they show some land-status detail (including Indian reserves and other private property, vacant Crown land, and parks) which helps you to know where to camp and where to find access to rivers. Crown land, as well as parkland, is open for public recreation. Many provincial maps are published in the 1:100,000 or the 1:125,000 series; the remaining ones are in the 1:250,000 series.

Federally produced maps in the 1:250,000 series cover the entire country. Eighty-four of them are required for complete coverage of British Columbia. In addition, the federal mapping and surveys branch makes a large-scale 1:50,000 series and a small-scale 1:500,000 series, both of which can be useful to whitewater boaters, as well as the extremely small-scale 1:1,000,000 International Map of the World series. The last-mentioned is numbered differently (under the world system), but is printed federally and sold by Canada Map Office. Another federal surveys and mapping branch offering of particular interest to river runners is the *Maps and Wilderness Canoeing* pamphlet. In addition to a listing of all map names and numbers in the 1:250,000 series, this free index contains useful tips on how to use topographic maps. Ask for it (MCR 107) from your map dealer or from Canada Map Office.

## Where to Obtain Topographic Maps, Air Photos, Tide Tables

Borrow maps: Complete sets of both federal and provincial maps are available for reference at a few locations; partial collections at others. Enquire at public libraries, and at university map libraries and geography departments.

Buy maps: Dealers sometimes sell both the federal and the provincial editions; or they may be bought by mail or in person from a government sales office. Depending on the type of map you want, contact either the provincial or the federal sales office. The price of most maps usually is $3 each wherever you buy them; however, dealers may set their own prices. Order maps by NTS name and number.

Buy air photos: Usually the largest-scale and the most up-to-date air photos are sold by the provincial government ($2 each). If you do not find what you want there, check federal air photos ($2.50 each).

Buy tide tables: *Canadian Tide & Current Tables, Volumes 5* and *6*, are available ($1.75 per volume) at most marine stores, some map outlets, and by mail or in person from:

Canadian Hydrographic Service
Chart Distribution Office
Institute of Fisheries and Oceans
P.O. Box 6000
9860 West Saanich Road,
Sidney, B.C. V8L 4B2
(604)656-8358
*For a complete list of dealers who sell Canadian Hydrographic Service nautical charts and related publications (tide tables) ask for the free* Pacific Coast Catalogue.

*Air photo of Woss: See Island Highway 19, the Nimpkish River, and the waterfall upstream from the bridge.*

## Topographic Map and Air-Photo Sales Outlets

A free Index 2 (to British Columbia maps in the NTS series) can be obtained from all map outlets. A compact set of air-photo indices (microfiche) can be seen at the offices of MAPS-B.C. in Victoria; at the B.C. Government Agency and at the Department of Geography, University of British Columbia, in Vancouver; at regional offices of the Ministry of Environment throughout British Columbia; and at the National Air Photo Library in Ottawa. If unable to visit a viewing station, ask MAPS-B.C. to mail (free) a photocopied portion of index to cover the area you are interested in along with instructions on how to order air photos. To make purchases by mail or in person contact:

MAPS-B.C.
Surveys and Mapping Branch
Parliament Buildings
Victoria, B.C. V8V 1X5
(604)387-1441
(Located in Room 110, 553 Superior Street)
*For provincial map and air-photo sales; a complete inventory*

B.C. Government Agency
222 Robson Square
800 Hornby Street
Vancouver, B.C. V6Z 2C5
(604)668-2654
*For provincial map and air-photo sales*

Geological Survey of Canada
Sales Information Office, 6th Floor
100 West Pender Street
Vancouver, B.C. V6B 1R0
(604)666-1271
*For federal maps of British Columbia; a complete inventory*

Canada Map Office
615 Booth Street
Ottawa, Ontario K1A 0E9
(613)998-9900
*For federal map sales, a list of dealers, and free* Maps and Wilderness Canoeing *pamphlet and index (MCR 107); a complete inventory*

Dominion Map Ltd.
541 Howe Street
Vancouver, B.C. V6C 2C2
(604)684-4341
*For provincial and federal map sales; also tide tables*

Renouf Books and Maps
522 West Hastings Street
Vancouver, B.C. V6B 1L6
(604)687-3320
*For federal maps and a few provincial maps; also tide tables*

National Air Photo Library
615 Booth Street
Ottawa, Ontario K1A 0E9
(613)995-4560
*For federal air photos; a complete inventory*

The above-named dealers stock the largest inventories of materials. Many more outlets sell a limited number of maps of the area in which they are located. A list of all federal topographic map dealers in British Columbia is available from Canada Map Office. To obtain provincial or federal maps or photos when in an outlying region, visit the local provincial Government Agent whose address and telephone number are in the Blue Pages of the telephone directory. If the map you want is not in stock, the Government Agent can take your payment, order by telephone from Victoria, and the map will be mailed to you.

# 5. RIVERFLOW INFORMATION

Federal and provincial governments collaborate to provide riverflow information: past, present, and future.

| | |
|---|---|
| Water Survey of Canada | Provincial Water Management Branch |
| Suite 502 | Ministry of Environment |
| 1001 West Pender Street | Parliament Buildings |
| Vancouver, B.C. V6E 2M9 | Victoria, B.C. V8V 1X5    (604)387-1111 |
| (604)666-3850 (after 1 p.m.) | (Located on 5th Floor, 765 Broughton Street) |

## Historical Data

All rivers for which Canadian riverflow records have been kept are listed in the *Surface Water Data Reference Index*. Monthly and annual mean discharges for the entire period of record of each river since riverflow measurement began in British Columbia in 1911 are in the *Historical Streamflow Summary* and in subsequent *Surface Water Data* annuals. These publications are compiled by Water Survey of Canada, and the extensive details in them are summarized in the hydrographs in this guidebook, and others in the series.

The hydrographs, however, provide only monthly averages. You might also want daily figures or those for a particular year, especially for flash rivers. Details on individual water-gauging stations, as well as recent figures not yet published, may be obtained from the Water Survey of Canada office. When asking for data, state the name and number of the water-gauging station and the year you are interested in, and request photocopies of the relevant data.

## Current Information

Current riverflow data are available by telephone for a limited number of rivers in British Columbia. At the time of writing, year-round daily reports are made on only one location in the province that is within, or near to, a run in this guidebook series; that one is the Thompson River near Spences Bridge, on which discharge figures are obtainable 24 hours a day. The reports are updated daily Monday through Friday at 8 a.m. on a recorded telephone message at (604)666-6087.

During spring runoff (from approximately March through June), freshet figures are reported for the following locations that relate to sites in this series of guidebooks: Fraser River at McBride, Kootenay River at Fort Steele, Mission Creek near East Kelowna, Similkameen River near Hedley, and the Thompson River near Spences Bridge. For current information on these stations telephone Water Survey of Canada office after 1 p.m. at (604)666-3850.

## Future Outlook

An idea of runoff to expect can be gleaned from the *Snow Survey Bulletin* published six times yearly (February 1 through June 1). These bulletins relate snowpack conditions to water-supply outlook. Every issue contains an easy-to-understand summary of information on snowpack, weather, and runoff. In addition, the April 1 and May 1 bulletins contain streamflow forecasts.

For more facts upon which the bulletins are based, also study the historical *Snow Survey Measurements Summary*. Both the bulletins and the summary are obtainable from the provincial Water Management Branch.

*Recording gauge beside Elk River, near Strathcona Park Lodge*

# WATER-GAUGING STATIONS
## on Vancouver Island

| River, Station Name, and Number (active or inactive) | Period of Record | Maximum Recorded Discharge and Date |
|---|---|---|
| Adam River (no station) | None | No records |
| Campbell River near Campbell River 08HD003 (inactive) | 22 years | 835 m$^3$/s (29,500 cfs) on November 15, 1953 |
| Chemainus River near Westholme 08HA001 (active) | 32 years | 457 m$^3$/s (16,100 cfs) on December 26, 1980 |
| Cowichan River at Lake Cowichan 08HA002 (active) | 47 years | 331 m$^3$/s (11,700 cfs) on January 21, 1968 |
| Davie River (no station) | None | No records |
| Eve River (no station) | None | No records |
| Gold River below Ucona River 08HC001 (active) | 24 years | 1890 m$^3$/s (66,700 cfs) on November 13, 1975 |
| Koksilah River at Cowichan Station 08HA003 (active) | 30 years | 212 m$^3$/s (7,500 cfs) on December 14, 1979 |
| Marble River at outlet of Alice Lake 08HE001 (inactive) | 11 years | 507 m$^3$/s (17,900 cfs) on January 1, 1927 |
| Nanaimo River near Cassidy 08HB034 (active) | 15 years | 958 m$^3$/s (33,800 cfs) on December 27, 1980 |
| Nimpkish River near Englewood 08HF002 (inactive) | 13 years | 1270 m$^3$/s (44,900 cfs) on December 31, 1926 |
| White River (no station) | None | No records |

# GLOSSARY OF SPECIAL TERMS USED BY RIVER RUNNERS AND SURFERS

**big water:** large-volume, turbulent water characterized by boils and whirlpools as well as big waves and holes. Heavy water is similar but less violent.

**boil:** water welling up into a mound; occurs in big water.

**bony:** description of a river at low volume with many rocks showing on which careful maneuvering is required to avoid hitting or scraping the rocks.

**boulder garden:** a boulder-strewn section of river.

**braided river:** a river split by sand or gravel bars into two or more channels that later converge and split again like a braid.

**break:** an ocean swell breaking into whitewater surf.

**broaching:** boat turning broadside to the river current and onto a rock or other obstacle; or boat turning broadside to the ocean surf.

**busy water:** water requiring a great deal of precision or maneuvering.

**C-1:** a decked canoe propelled by one person in a kneeling position using a single-bladed paddle.

**C-2:** a decked canoe propelled by two persons in a kneeling position, each using a single-bladed paddle.

**canoe:** see open-Canadian canoe, closed-canoe, C-1 and C-2.

**cascade:** water coursing over a series of ledges or boulders; almost a waterfall.

**channel:** water flowing through a deeper part of the riverbed or a river route where a boat can go.

**chicken route:** a relatively easier way down the river.

**chute:** a channel in which fast water flows through a navigable gap in a drop.

**clean break:** an ocean swell that starts breaking at one end and continues breaking evenly and smoothly in a line horizontal to the shore while also rolling in toward the beach.

**clean river:** a river that is normally free from sweepers and logjams.

**closed-boat:** a decked whitewater craft (kayak or C-1 or C-2).

**closed-canoe:** a decked boat paddled by one or two persons in a kneeling position, each using a single-bladed paddle.

**curl:** the breaking part of a wave in ocean surf.

**continuous rapids:** water flowing without stopping.

**cushion:** water piling up on the upstream side of a rock or other obstacle.

**dam:** a man-made barrier across a river that holds back the water. Often it is used to regulate the flow by allowing water to pass through it, or around it, but water does not flow over it.

**drop-and-pool river:** a river in which still pools alternate with whitewater drops.

**drop:** a section of river, usually short, where the water descends relatively rapidly between two flatter stretches of water.

**dumper:** an ocean surf wave that breaks abruptly close to shore and pounds you onto the beach; it is formed because the shore drops steeply.

**eddy:** a resting place in a flowing stream where the water is still or the current flows upstream; an area of slack water downstream from a riverbend, a rock, or other obstruction in the river where it is possible to stop.

**eddy-hop:** proceed downriver, across it, or upstream by moving from eddy to eddy and using each eddy to slow down or stop to scout, or to play.

**eddy fence:** a wall of water along the eddy line between the mainstream and the eddy; usually occurs in big water.

**ender (endo):** a maneuver — purposeful or accidental — in which the boat flips end over end, either forward or backward. It occurs on big, steep ocean surf, and in deep holes and on the upstream side of large standing waves on rivers.

**Eskimo rescue:** a technique whereby a paddler in an upright kayak assists a buddy in an overturned kayak to become upright. The paddler in the overturned kayak beats the bottom of the boat to call for help, and the rescuer responds by placing his or her boat at right angles to the center of the overturned boat so that the upset paddler can grasp the bow and use it to become upright.

**Eskimo roll:** maneuver in which a closed-boater, remaining in an overturned kayak or decked canoe, uses a paddle and a hip-flick body motion to right the craft.

**ferrying:** a technique for crossing the current by angling the boat while paddling upstream.

**flash rivers:** rain-fed (sometimes snow-melt) rivers that rise and fall quickly.

**frowning hole:** a horseshoe-shaped drop that looks as if it is frowning (with a down-turned mouth) when viewed from upstream. This hole formation is more likely to be a dangerous keeper (see *keeper* listing) than is a smiling hole or a ledge drop.

**gradient:** the average amount that a river drops expressed in meters/kilometer (feet/mile).

**the green:** smooth ocean swells, usually beyond the surf break.

**glacial-melt:** description of a river that is sustained by the melting of glaciers. Normally these rivers reach large volume from mid-July to late September when the sun is hot.

**haystacks:** high, pointed standing waves.

**head wall:** a vertical rock wall or hard riverbank at a sharp bend in the river, often at a right angle. When the current is strong there will be a cushion of water on the wall, and often the wall is undercut.

**heavy water:** large-volume, turbulent water. Big water is similar but more violent.

**hole:** turbulent water on the downstream side of a submerged rock (or other obstacle) that is formed by the water flowing so swiftly over the rock that the water curls back on itself and then flows down to the riverbed. Sometimes a hole is called a reversal. Also see *keeper*.

**hotdogging:** playing in holes, eddies, and surfing waves to purposefully do pop-ups, enders, and other stunts on the water.

**house rock:** a very large rock or boulder, usually at least 3 meters (10 feet) high.

**hydraulics:** when used by whitewater boaters, this term refers to powerful waves, boils, whirlpools, and squirrelly, unpredictable surges of water found in large-volume rivers. Rollers, holes, reversals: "A thing that'll getcha."

**K-1:** a kayak for one person.

**K-2:** a kayak for two persons that is normally used on flat water.

**kayak:** a decked boat propelled by one or two persons from a sitting position, each using a double-bladed paddle.

**keeper:** a hole, or reversal, so powerful that it prevents a boat or a swimmer from leaving it. Holes formed below weirs or below bedrock ledges that are straight across become keepers with a lesser amount of water than does either a frowning hole or a smiling hole.

**ledge:** a horizontal rocky shelf, often at right angles to the current, over which the river drops abruptly; a hole formed on the down-stream side of it is likely to become a keeper at higher water.

**lining:** pulling a boat upstream or downstream, guiding it with ropes attached to the bow or stern, or to both.

**logjam:** logs, branches, and debris piled up in the river with water straining through them and flowing beneath them; potentially one of the most dangerous hazards on rivers.

**open-Canadian canoe:** a canoe without a deck paddled by one or two persons in a kneeling position, each using a single-bladed paddle.

**open-canoe:** a canoe without a deck paddled by one or two persons in a kneeling position, each using a single-bladed paddle.

**piling up:** a description of water rising on the river.

**pillow:** water piling up on a rock and just barely covering it. If you are just learning to kayak, heed this vivid warning I had from those who taught me: "If you see something downstream that is smooth and round and looks like a pillow, it's filled with rocks!"

**playing:** maneuvering for fun, often repeatedly in the same patch of white water; going into standing waves or surfing waves, riding a hole, or doing pop-ups or enders on purpose.

**play spot:** a hole, a series of surfing waves, or any other water that offers the possibility for play.

**pogies:** covers that fit over your hands and paddle to protect your hands from the wind; usually made of nylon material with Velcro closures to secure them.

**pop-up:** a hotdog maneuver performed purposefully — or accidentally — in which the bow, or stern, of a closed-boat drops vertically into the trough of a wave, or hole, and then forcefully pops up, sometimes clearing the water; a paddler with good balance can remain upright while doing this.

**portage:** the act of carrying boat and gear over land around a portion of river that the paddler does not want to run.

**put-in:** the launching point where you go onto the ocean surf or onto the river.

**raft:** an inflatable open boat that has a great deal of flotation and is rowed or paddled down the river.

**rain-fed:** description of a river having rainfall as its primary source. Rivers fed by rain can rise at any time of the year, but those at lower altitudes usually are high in winter.

**rapid (or rapids):** a portion of river where the water flows over obstructions, causing waves and turbulent water.

**reading water:** looking at the water to guess what is beneath the surface, to decide where the power is and how to use that power, and to choose a route down the river.

**riffles:** small, ripply waves.

**river left:** the left side of the river as the paddler is facing downstream.

**river right:** the right side of the river as the paddler is facing downstream.

**rock garden:** a shallow portion of river that is scattered with many visible rocks.

**roll:** see Eskimo roll.

**roller:** a large wave that is breaking, or rolling, upstream toward you.

**rooster tail:** spray at the top of a haystack wave.

**runoff:** surface water flowing off the land into creeks, rivers, and the sea. Sources are rainfall, melting snow, and melting glaciers.

**scouting:** looking ahead on the river, from your boat or by climbing onto shore and walking downstream, to study the water.

**shuttle:** transporting paddlers, boats, and gear between the put-in and the take-out.

**smiling hole:** a horseshoe-shaped drop which looks as if it were smiling (with up-turned lips) when viewed from upstream. It is less likely to be a keeper than is a "frowning hole", or especially a ledge that is straight across.

**sneaking:** the act of boating an easier route to by-pass a more difficult section of river.

**snow-melt:** description of a river which is sustained by melting snow; rivers with melting snow as a primary source are swollen in spring and in early summer during runoff.

**squirrelly water:** swirly, unpredictable hydraulics, usually occurring in medium-volume to large-volume rivers.

**staircase:** a series of ledge drops.

**standing waves:** waves that come in a series at the bottom of a drop where the river flattens and slows down.

**stopper:** a hole or a steep wave that momentarily stops a boat but does not keep it.

**strainer:** a sweeper or a fallen tree with branches hanging into the river and water flowing between them. Or, a gravel bar with small rocks scattered along its edge and water flowing between them: the latter type of strainer is usually deepest at either the upstream or the downstream end, and shallowest at its center.

**surfing (ocean):** riding the waves into shore.

**surfing (river):** coasting on a wave while facing upstream against the direction of the flowing current.

**sweeper:** a branch or tree extending from shore into the river right on the surface or just beneath it; potentially one of the most dangerous hazards found on rivers.

**take-out:** the point where you complete a run and leave the river.

**technical water:** this is water that requires precise maneuvering. Usually the term "technical" is used to describe smaller-volume, rocky streams; however, it also is used sometimes to describe heavy water requiring precision.

**tight:** description of a section of river in which precise maneuvering is required because the route or routes that can be taken are narrow and severely limited.

**toggles:** sticks attached to grab loops at the bow and stern of the boat; advisable to have them when ocean surfing. If you have to swim, they will save your hands from being twisted in the grab loops.

**tributary:** a smaller stream entering a larger one.

**waterfall:** flowing water in a river that drops freely, or very steeply.

**water-gauging station:** a place at the edge of the river where riverflow is measured by a staff gauge (which is read by someone) or measured by a recording gauge.

**weir:** a natural or man-made barrier across a river that might hold back water, but that normally allows water to flow over it; sometimes regulated. Weirs usually are so straight across that even when the drop is only a short distance a dangerous keeper is formed at the bottom of them.

**whirlpool:** a swirling vortex of water.

# INDEX TO PLACES, WHITEWATER TRIPS, FEATURES AND CONDITIONS, ACTIVITIES, AND FACILITIES

Betty Pratt-Johnson

# 141 DIVES

in the protected waters of Washington
and British Columbia

NEW UPDATED EDITION

**ANOTHER GUIDEBOOK BY
BETTY PRATT-JOHNSON**

*MORE THAN 20,000 COPIES SOLD*